# mandalas

## TO MY FUTURE MOTHER

Relax and Unwind with Gorgeous Mandalas: An Adult Coloring Book for Stress Relief

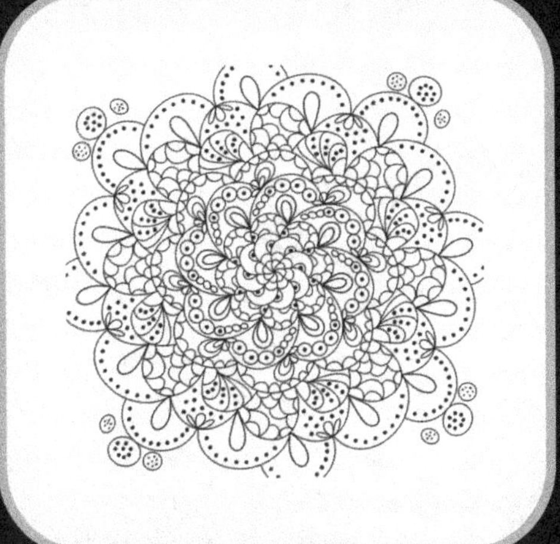

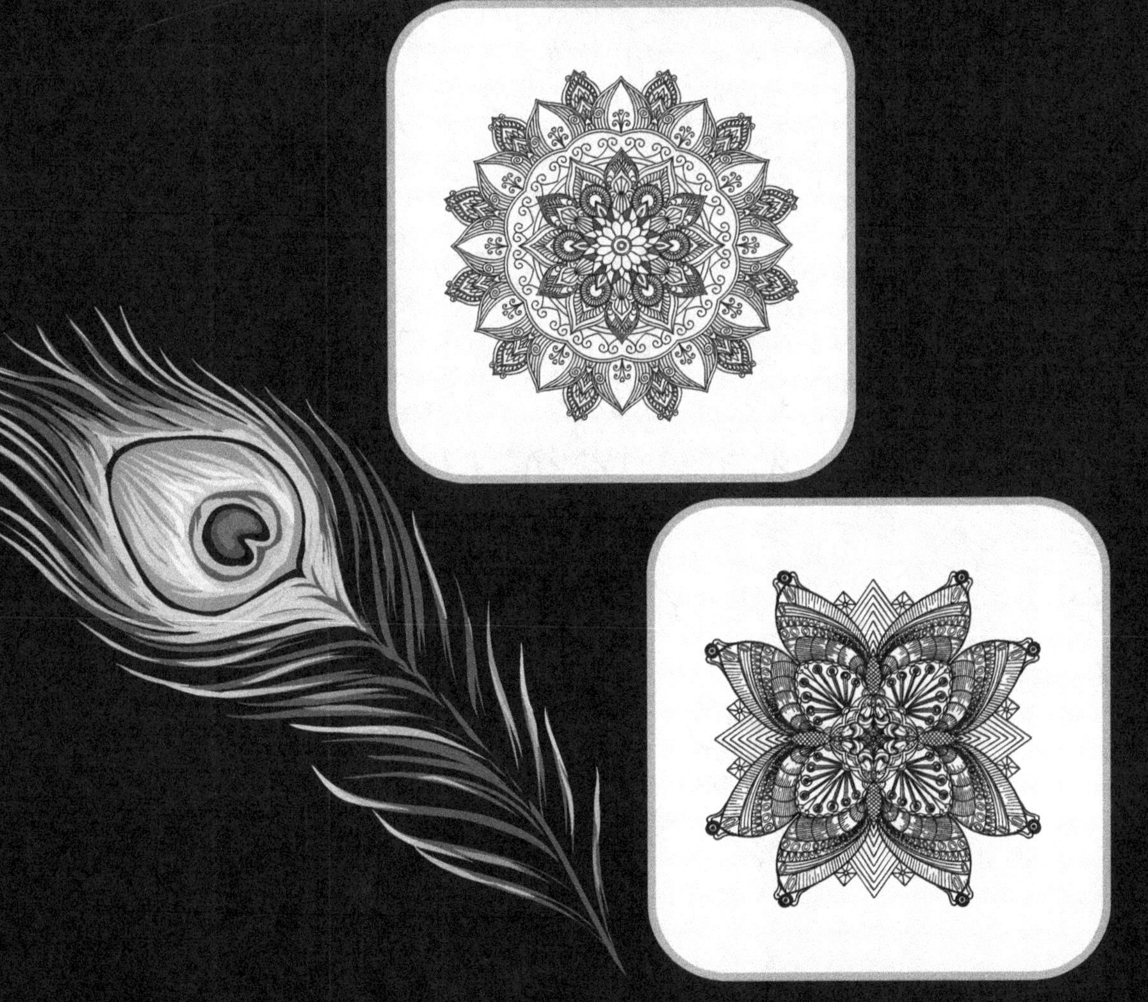

Abo Alaa

INTERNATIONAL DESIGNERDD

# Mama mandala

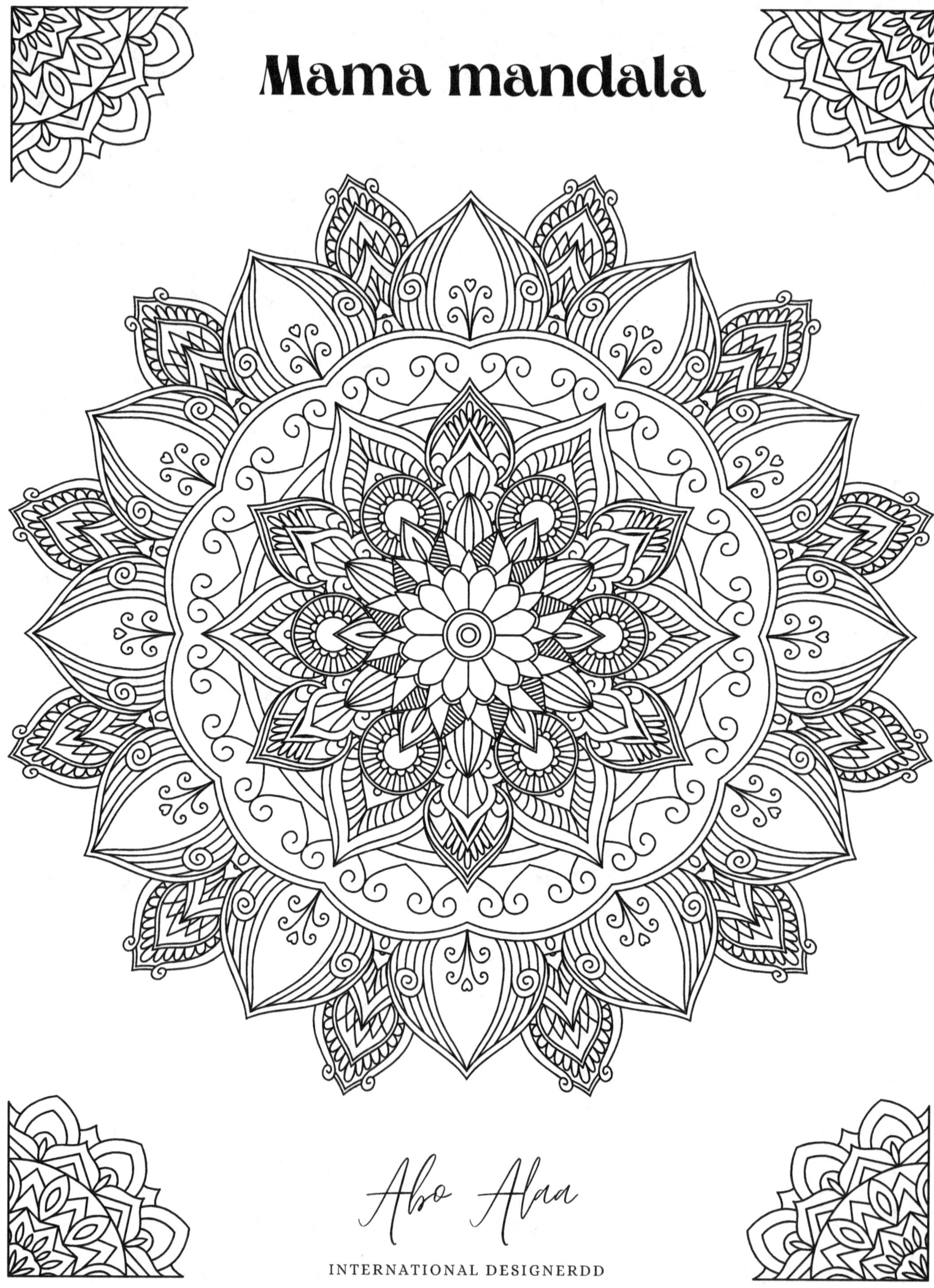

# Abo Alaa

## INTERNATIONAL DESIGNERDD

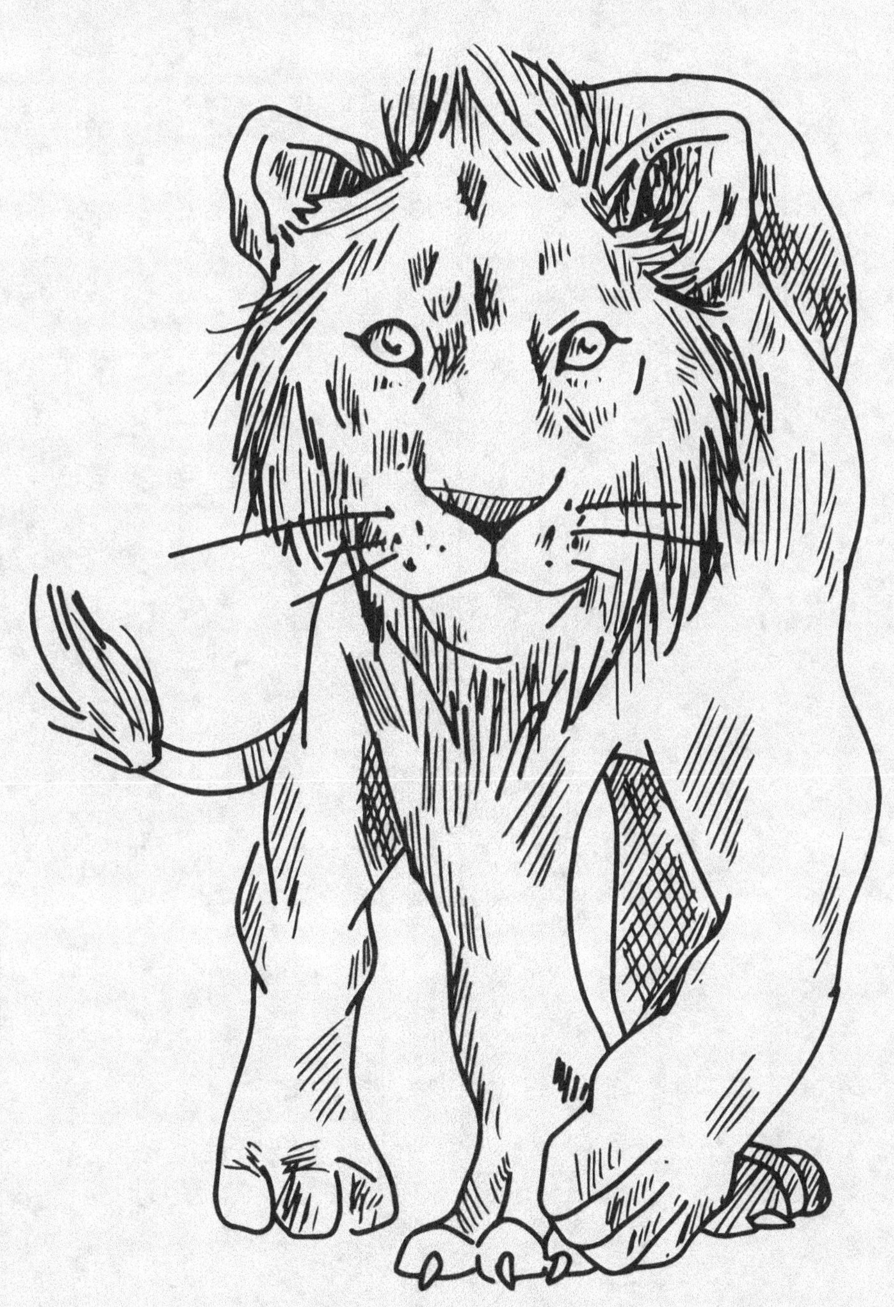

# Abo Alaa

INTERNATIONAL DESIGNERDD

# Mama mandala

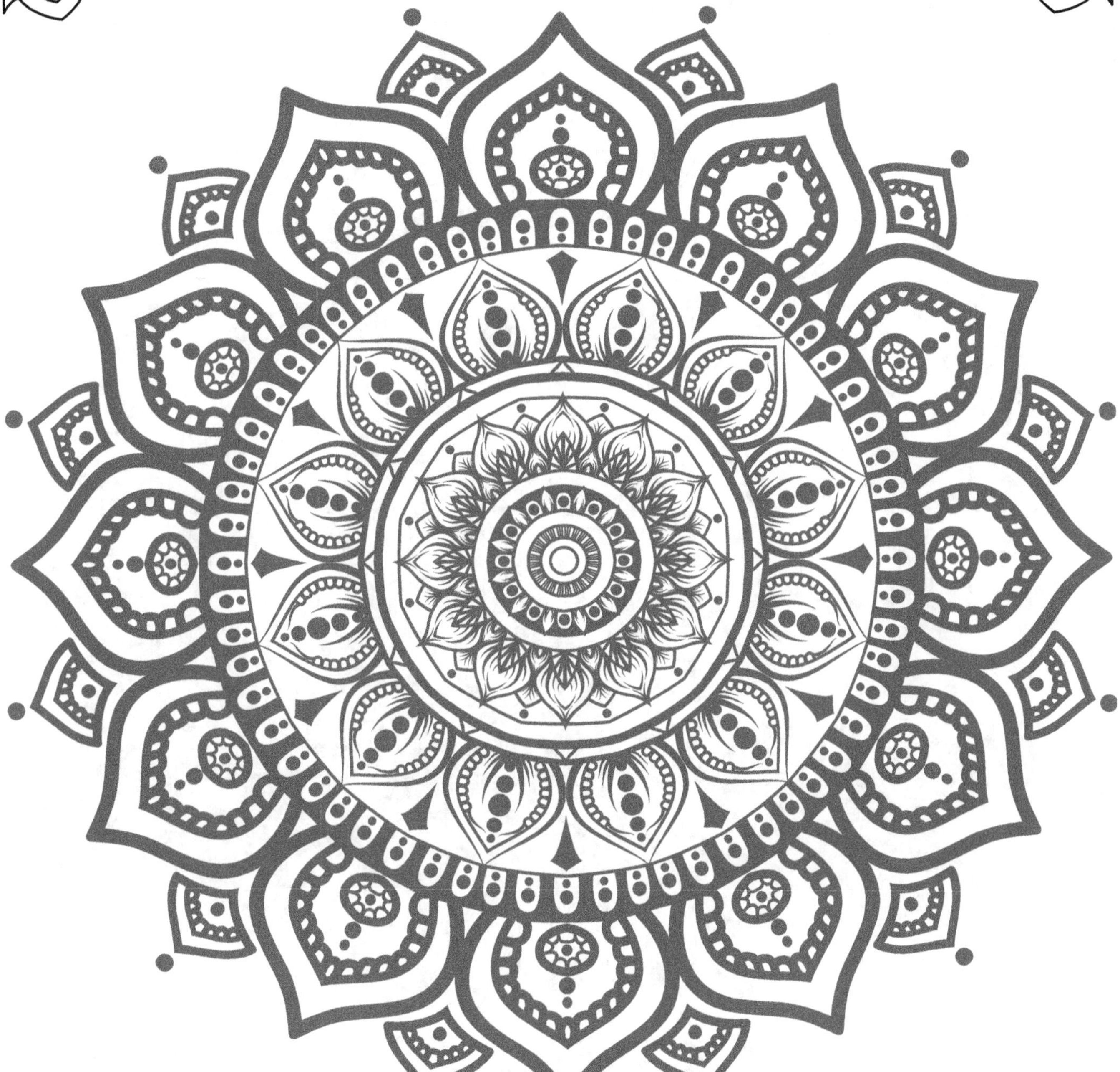

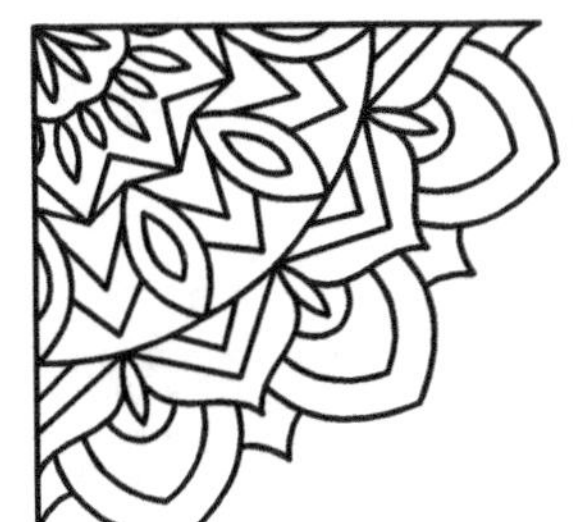
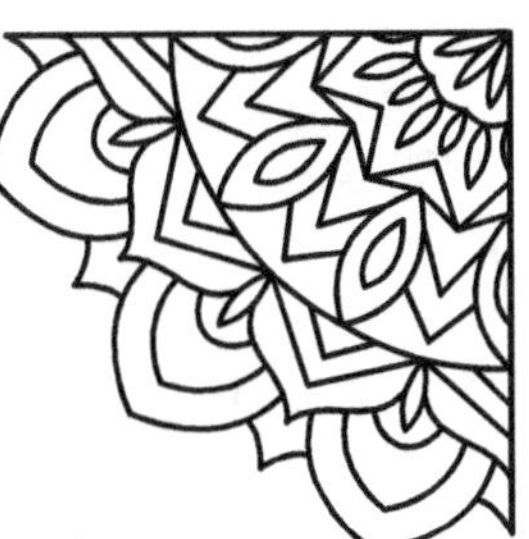
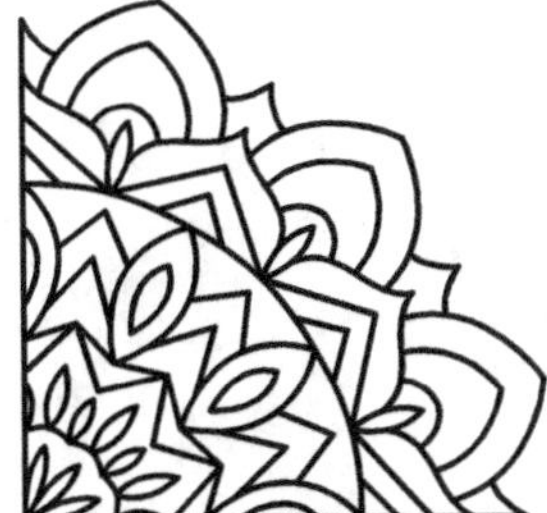
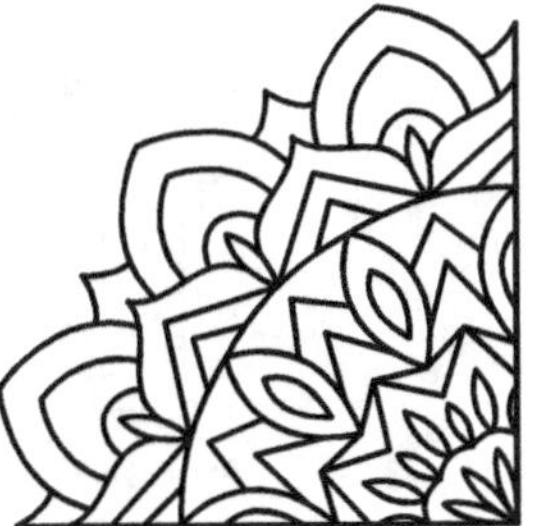

# Abo Alaa

INTERNATIONAL DESIGNERDD

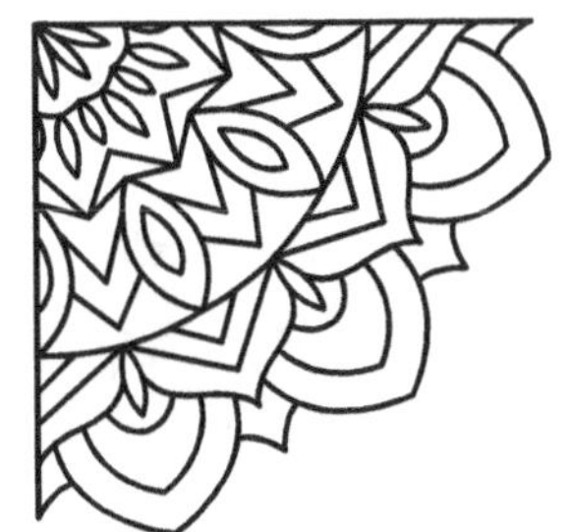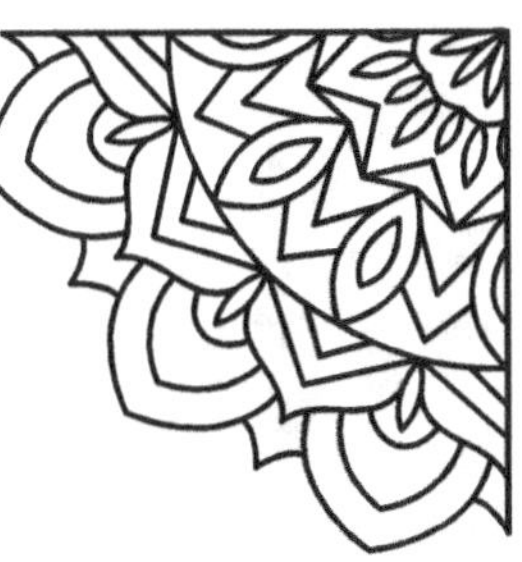

# Mama mandala

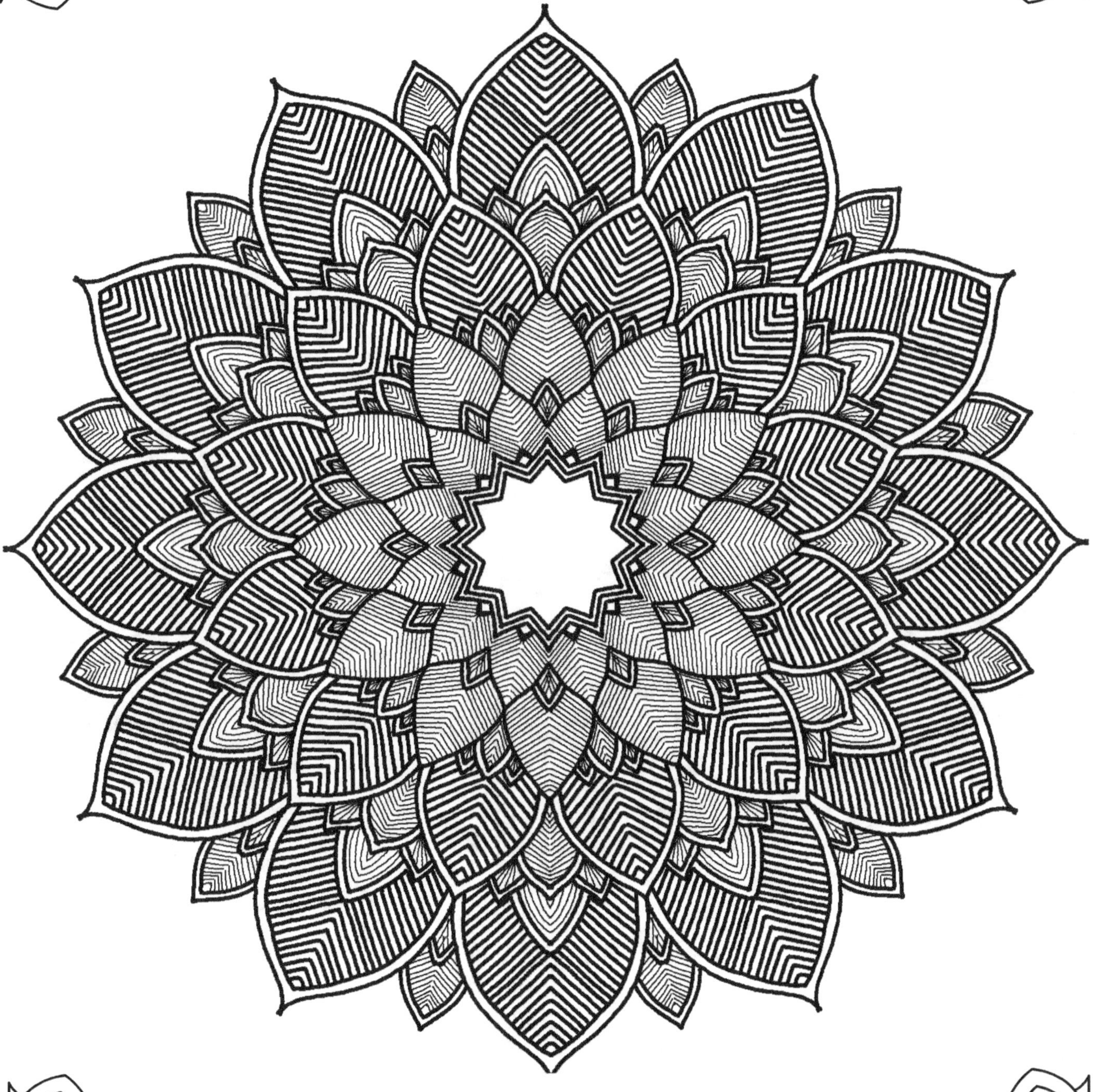

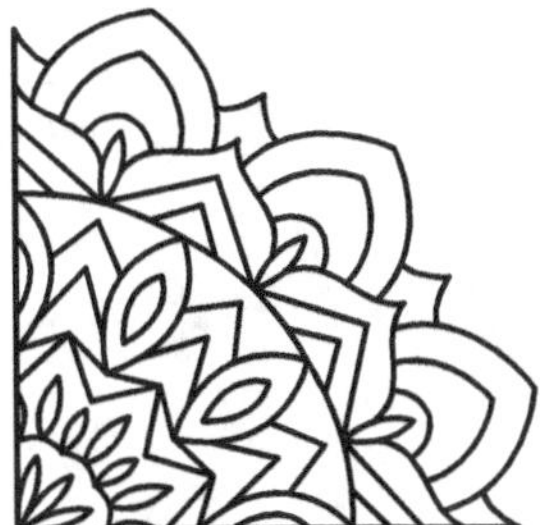

Abo Alaa

INTERNATIONAL DESIGNERDD

# Abo Alaa

INTERNATIONAL DESIGNERDD

# Mama mandala

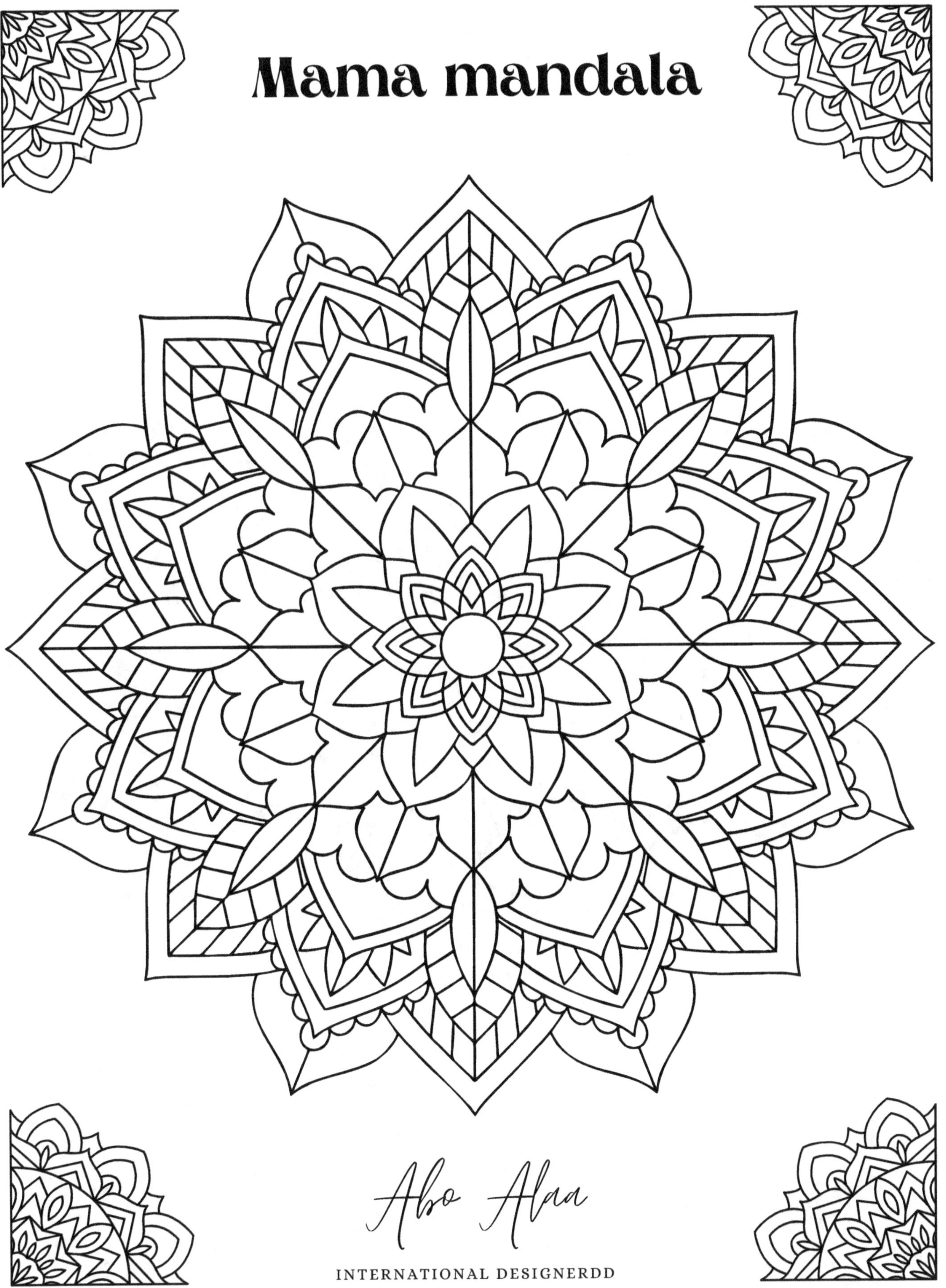

# Abo Alaa

INTERNATIONAL DESIGNERDD

# Mama mandala

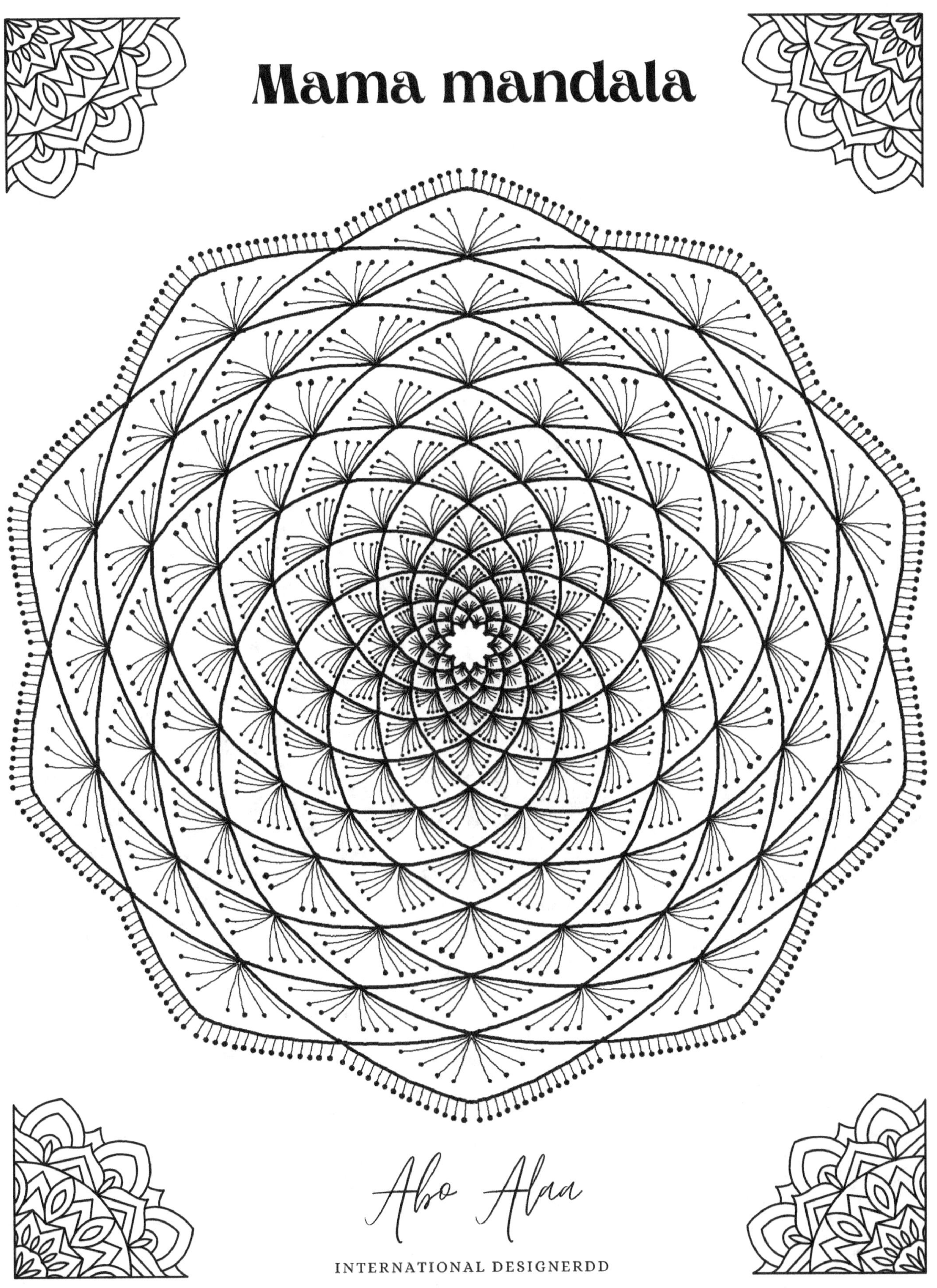

# Abo Alaa

INTERNATIONAL DESIGNERDD

# Mama mandala

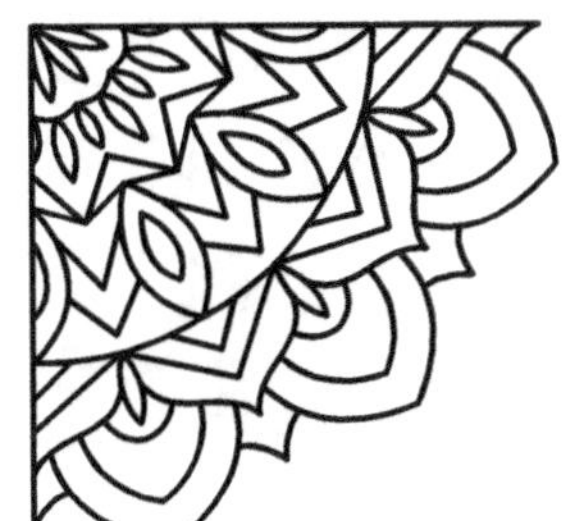
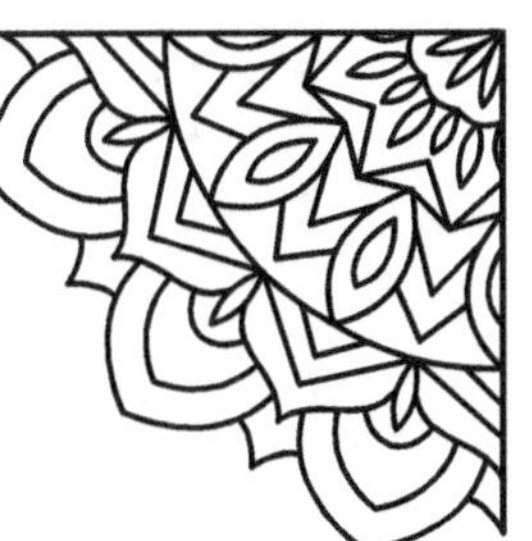
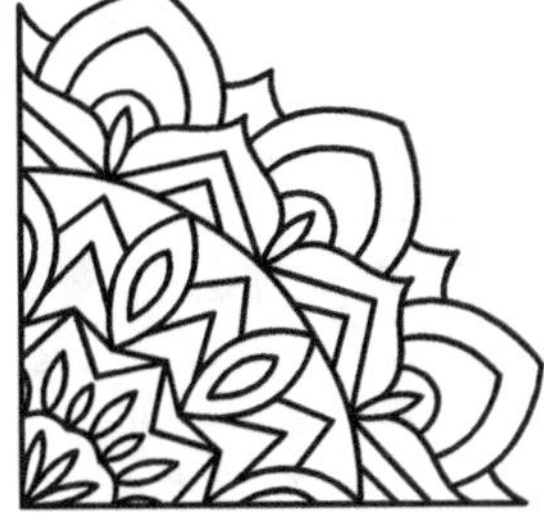
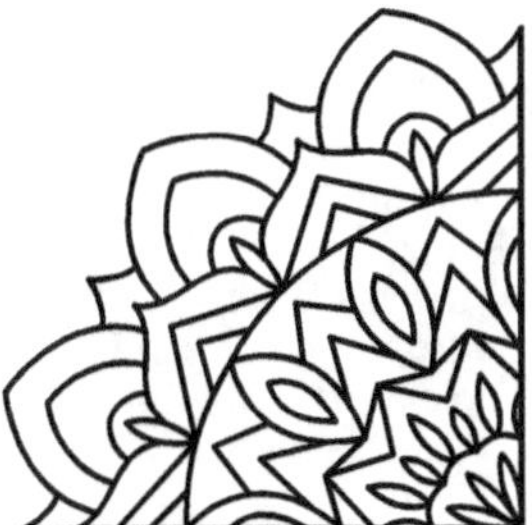

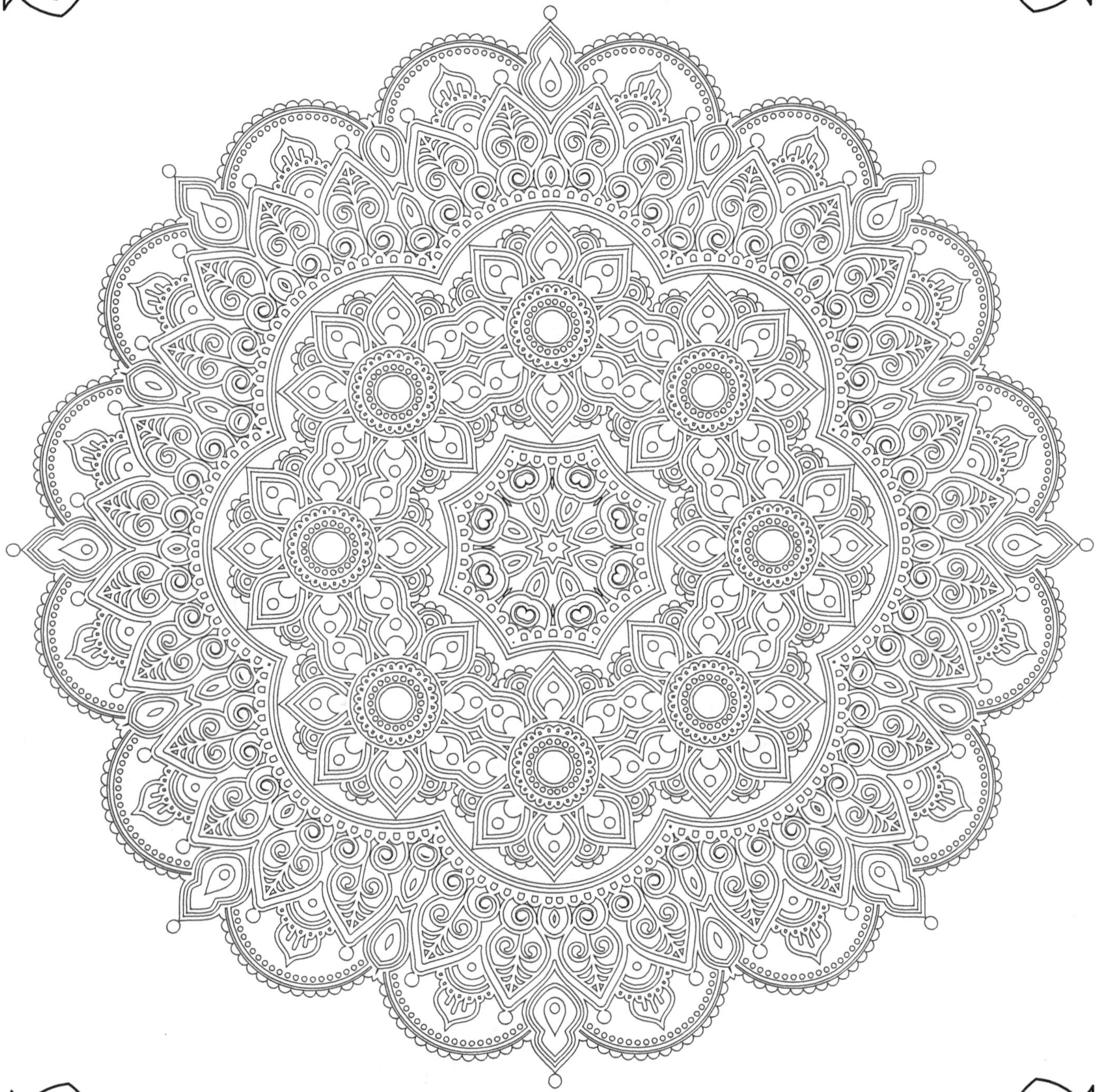

Abo Alaa

INTERNATIONAL DESIGNERDD

$Abo\ Alaa$

INTERNATIONAL DESIGNERDD

# Mama mandala

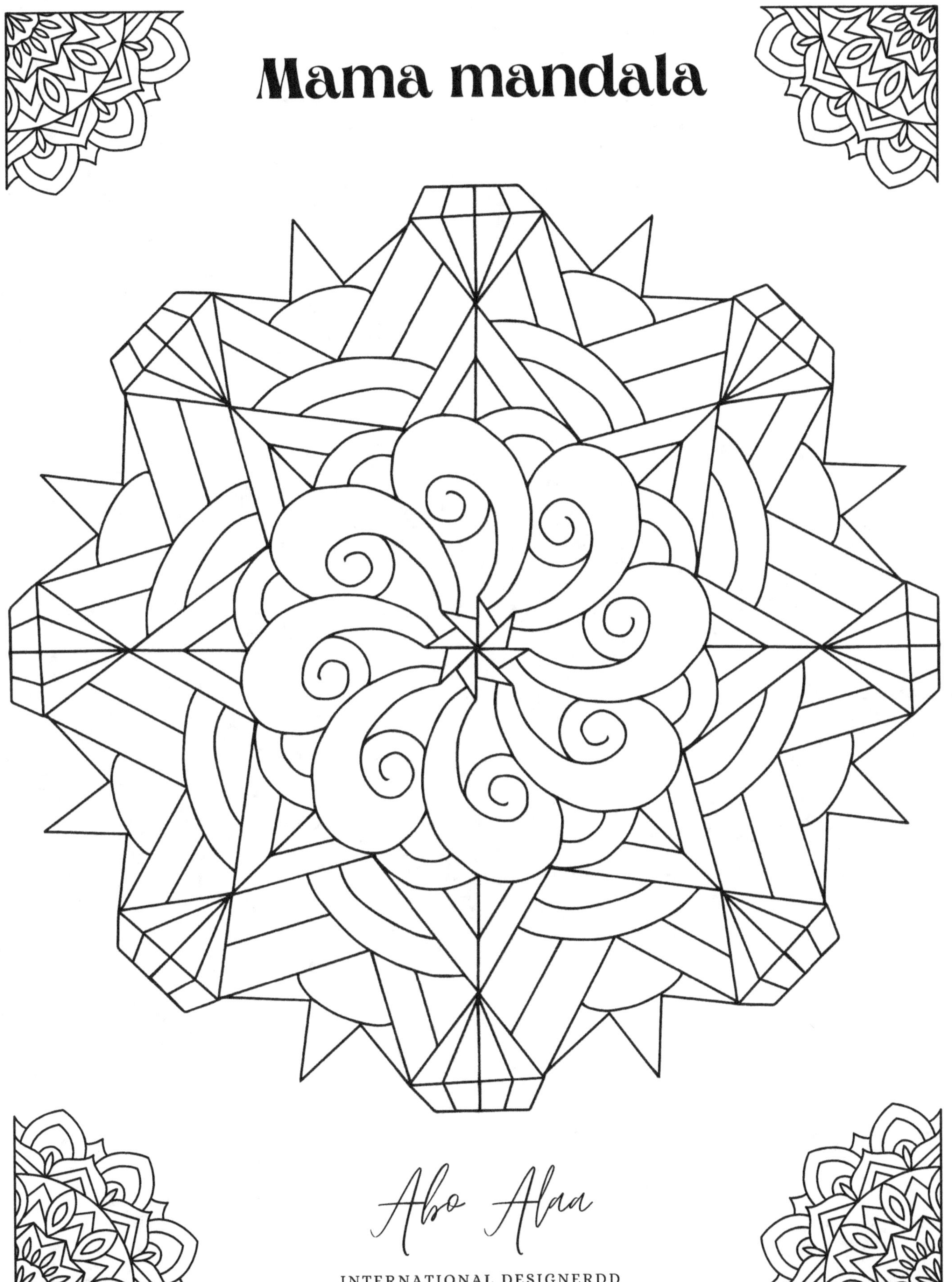

Abo Alaa

INTERNATIONAL DESIGNERDD

# Mama mandala

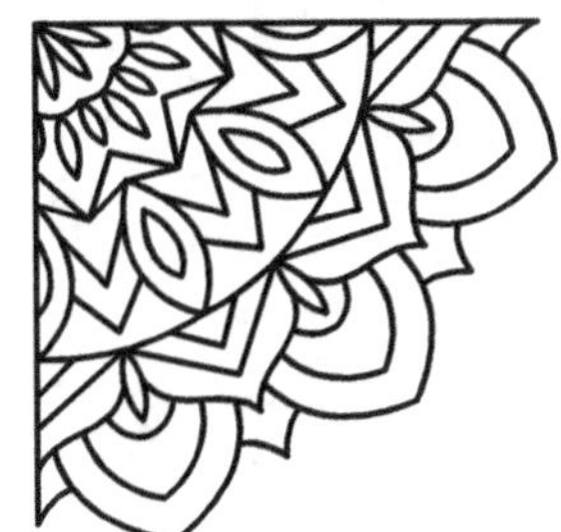
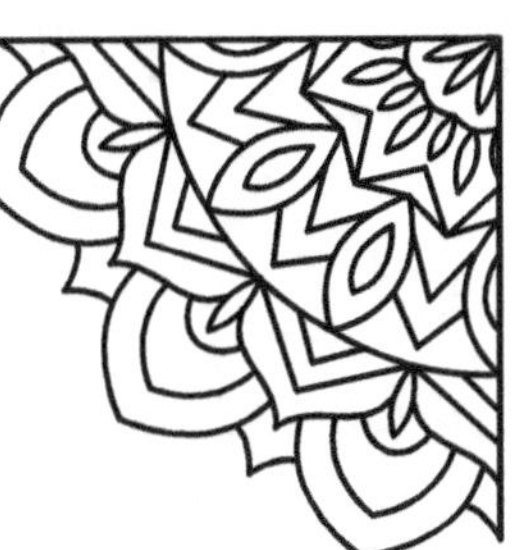
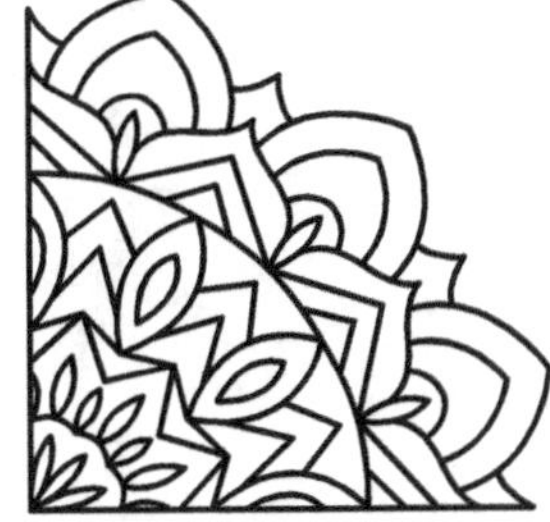
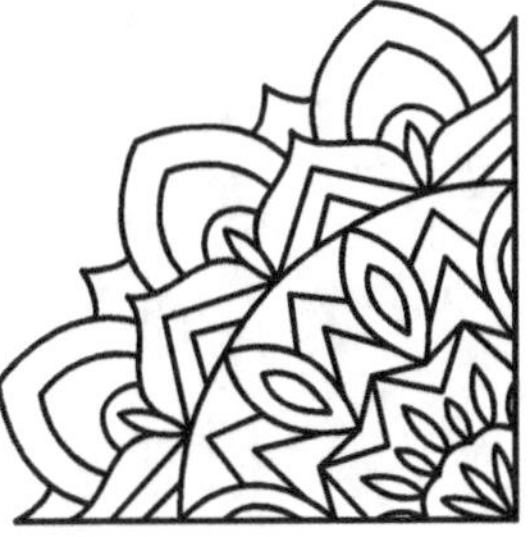

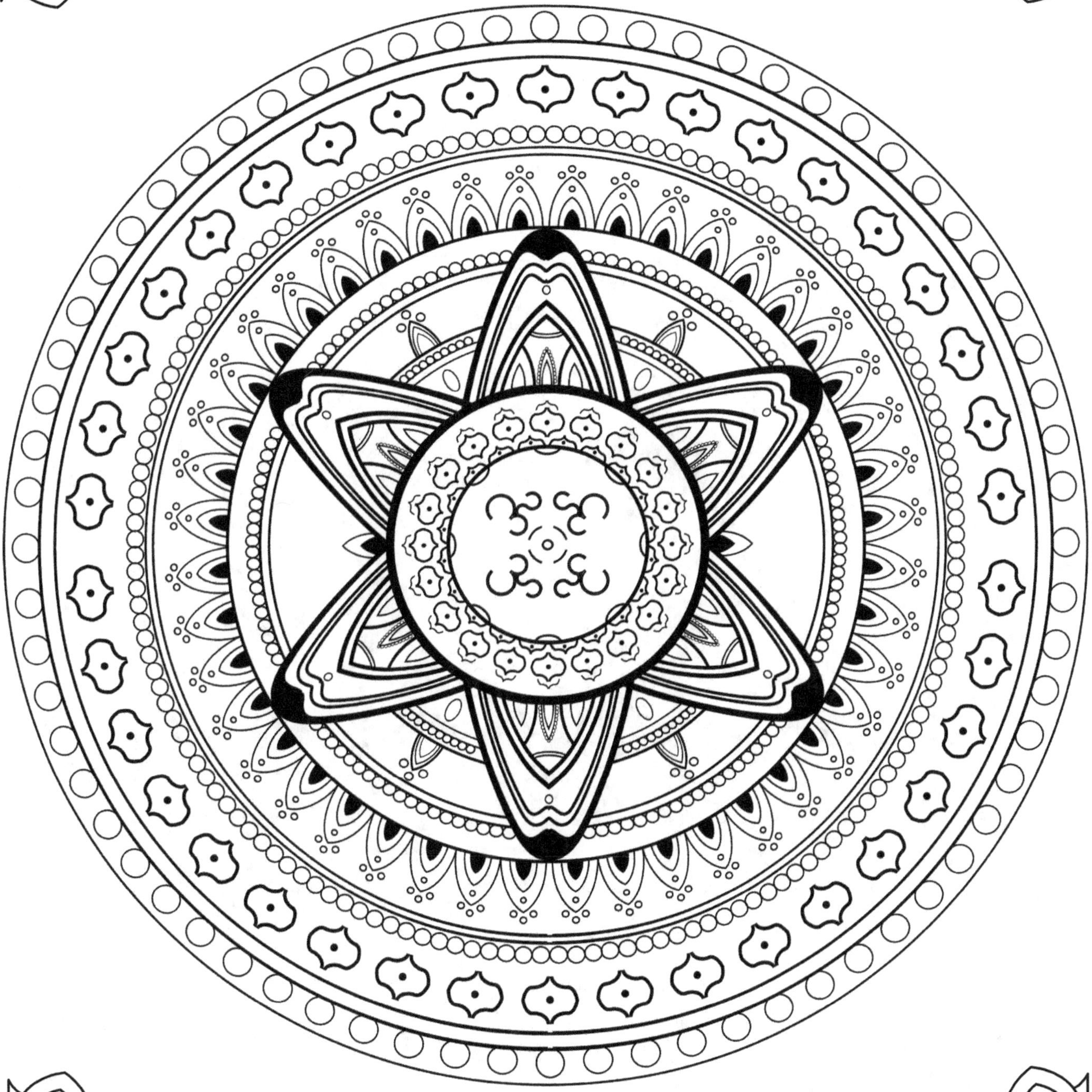

Abo Alaa

INTERNATIONAL DESIGNERDD

# Abo Alaa

INTERNATIONAL DESIGNERDD

# Mama mandala

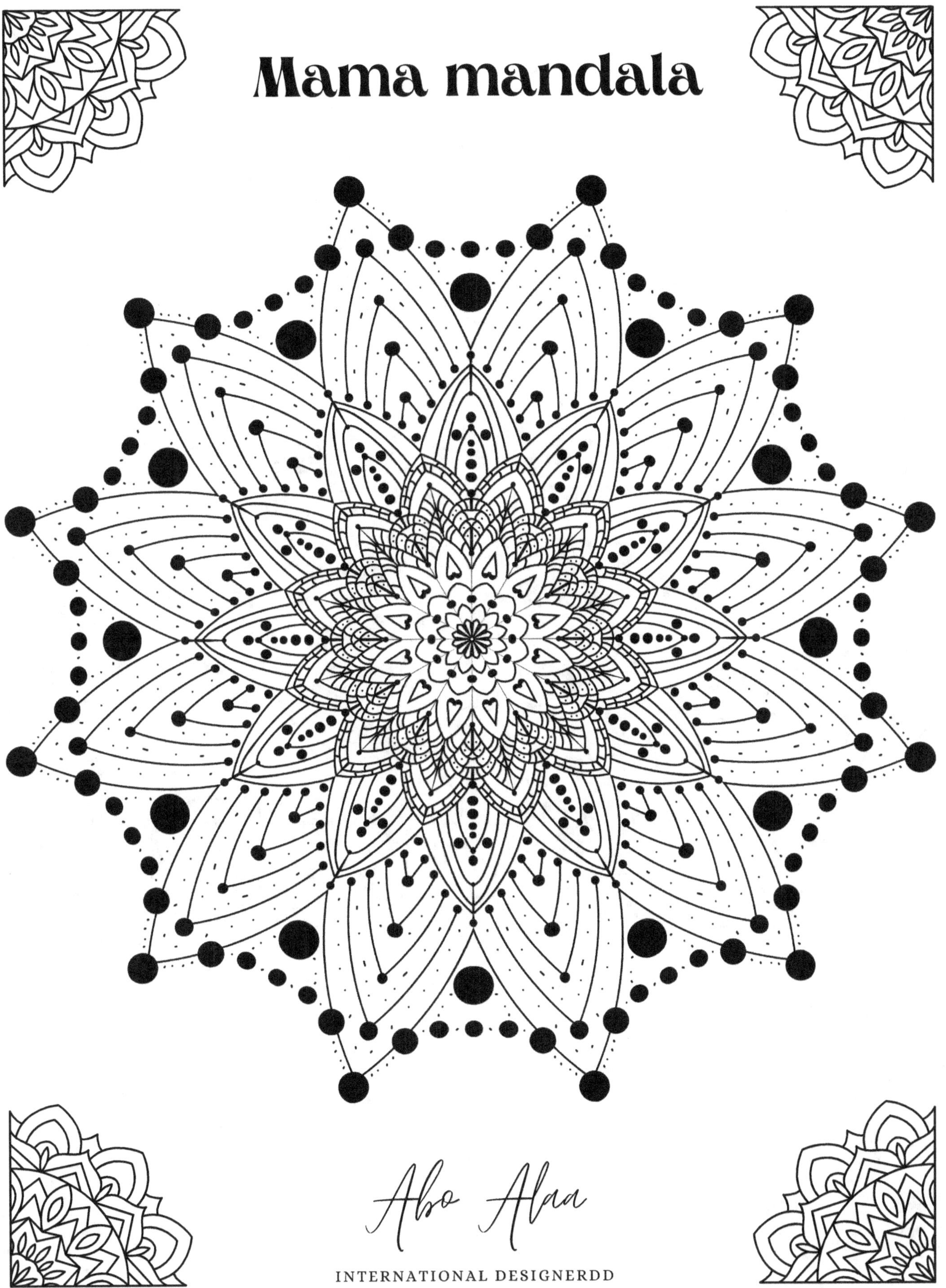

# Abo Alaa

INTERNATIONAL DESIGNERDD

# Mama mandala

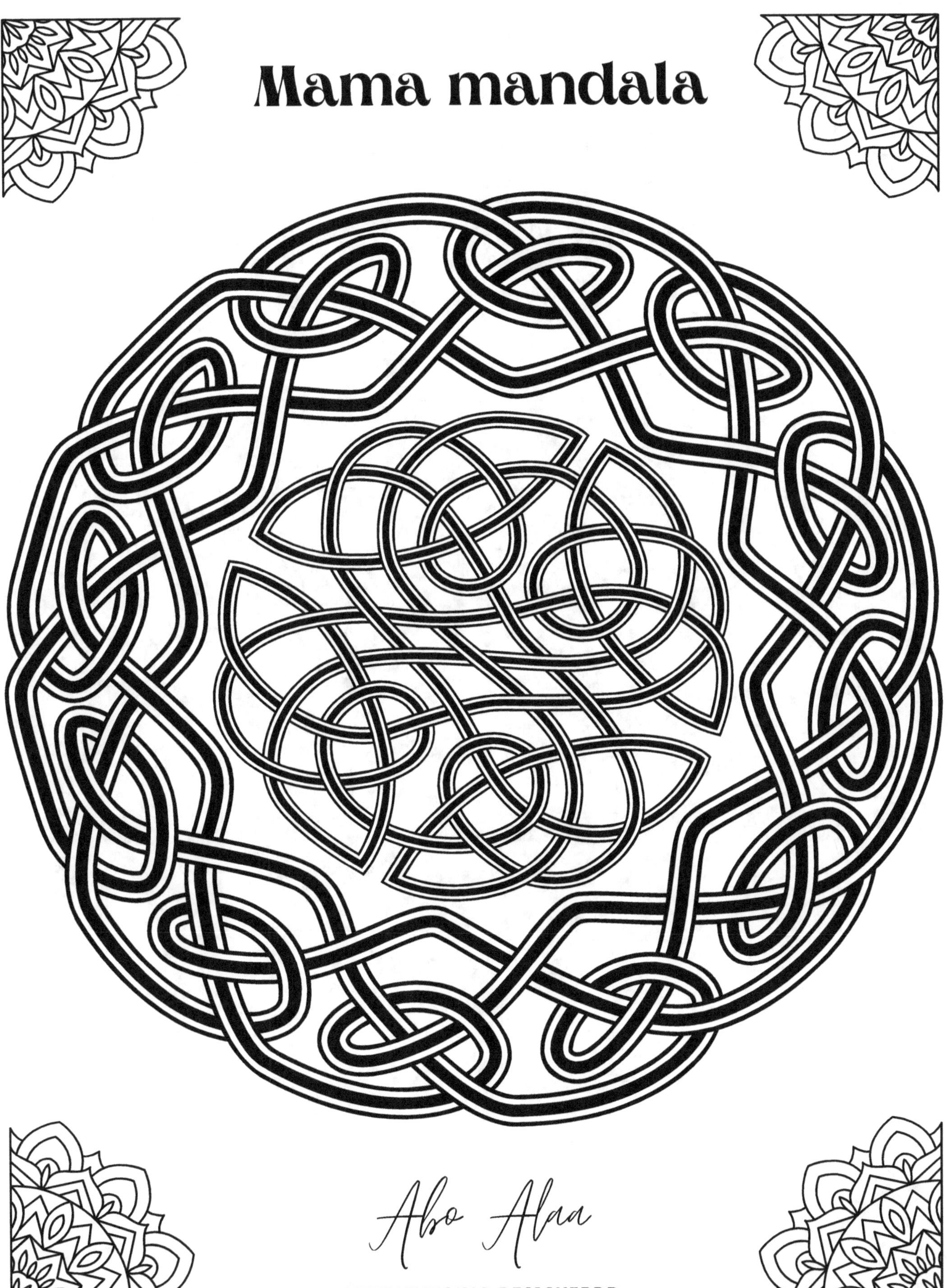

# Abo Alaa

INTERNATIONAL DESIGNERDD

# Mama mandala

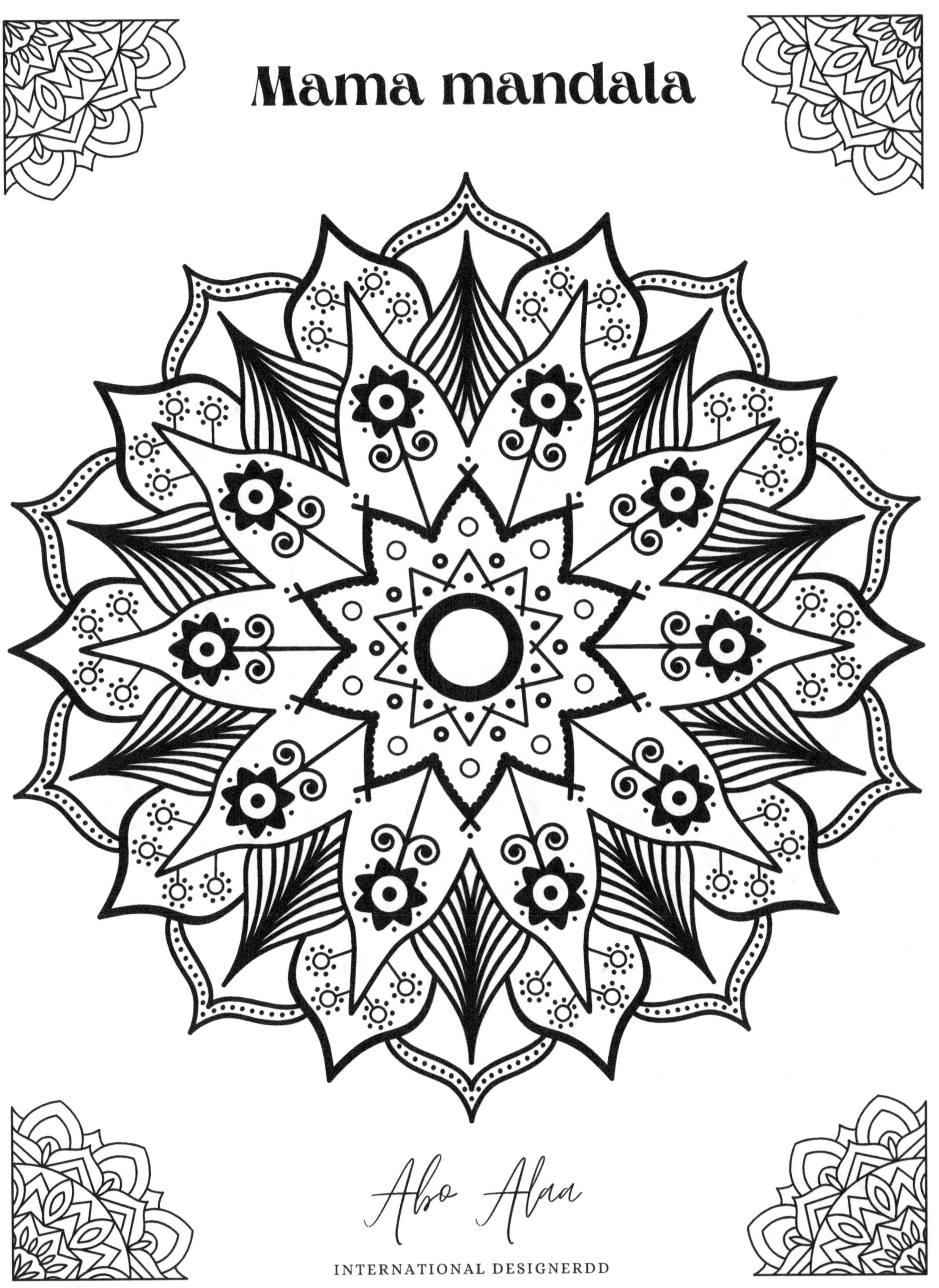

# Abo Alaa

INTERNATIONAL DESIGNERDD

# Mama mandala

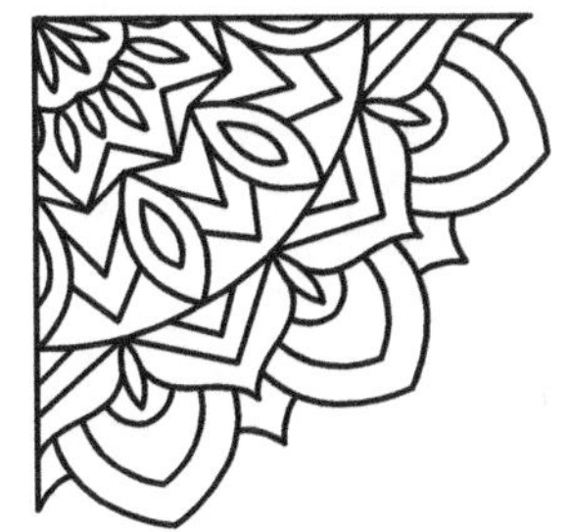
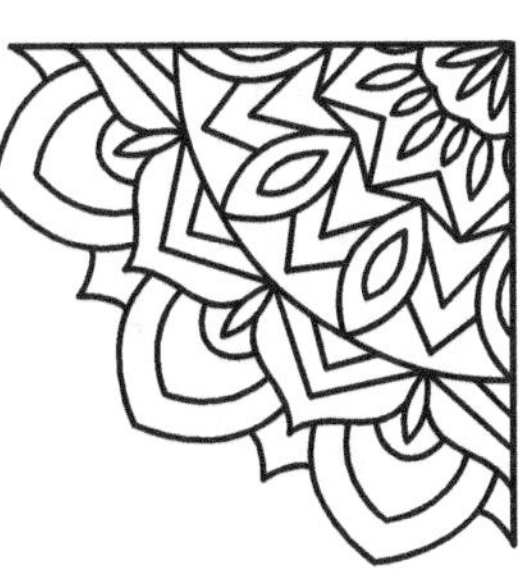
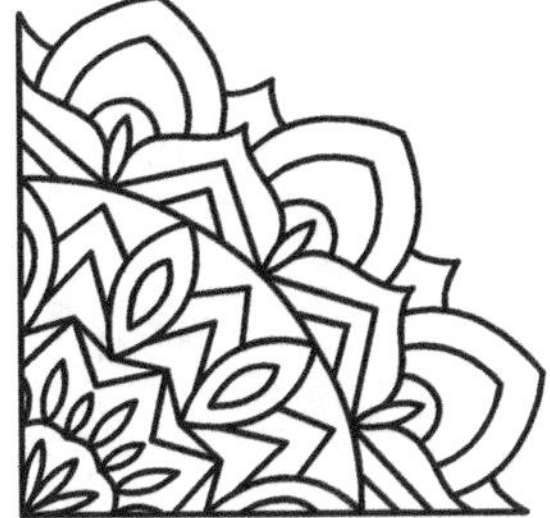

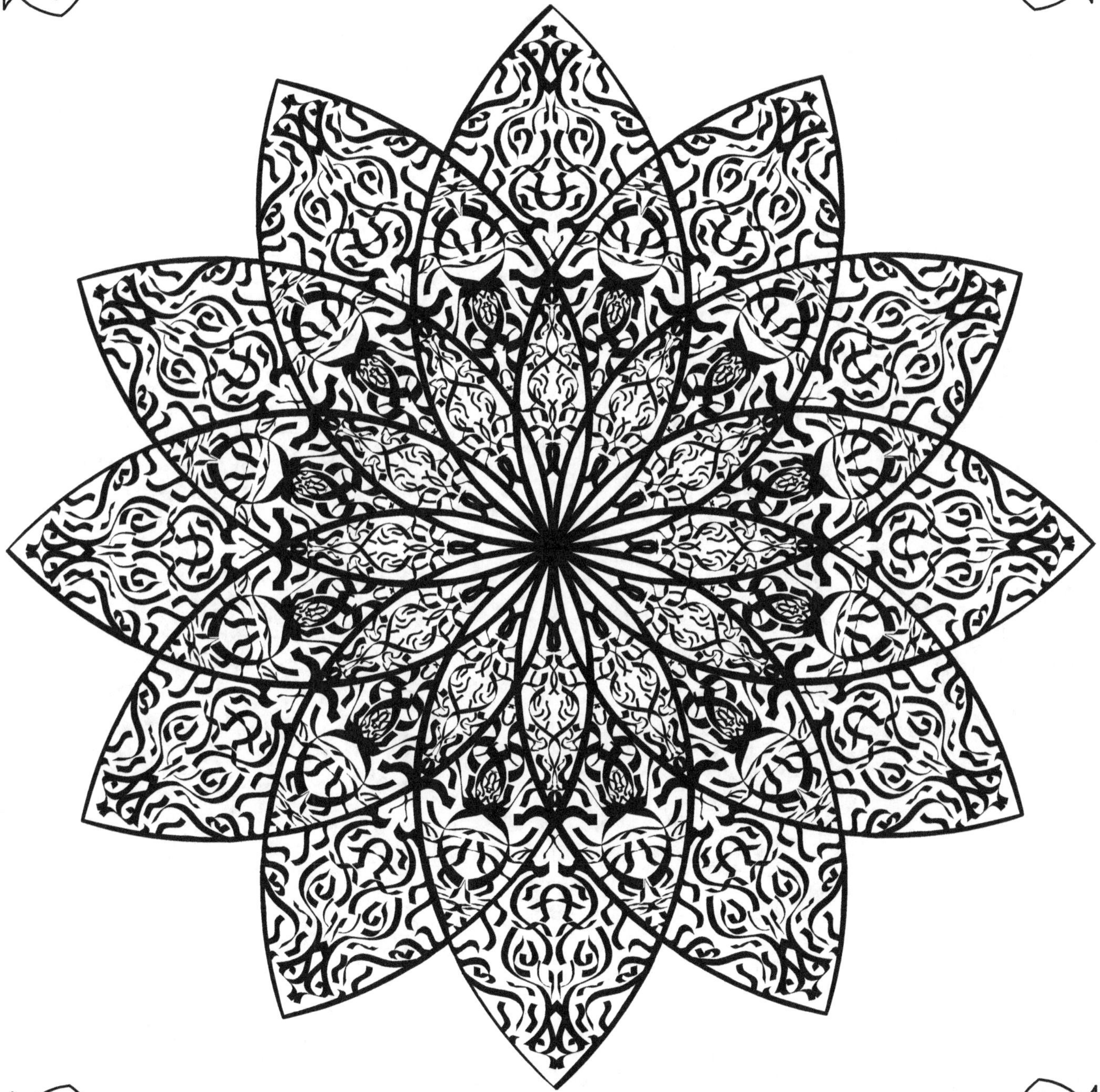

Abo Alaa

INTERNATIONAL DESIGNERDD

Abo Alaa
INTERNATIONAL DESIGNERDD

# Mama mandala

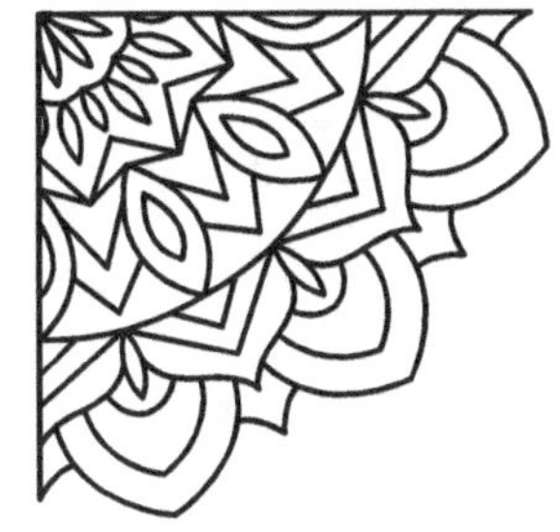
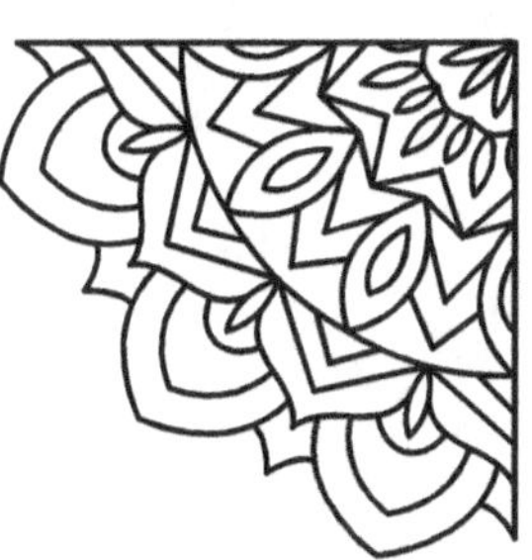
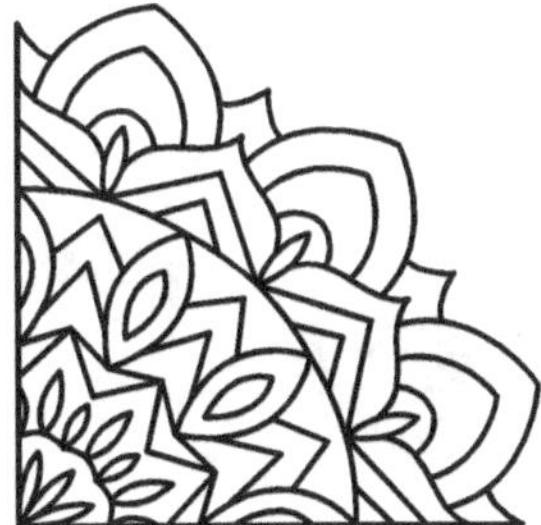

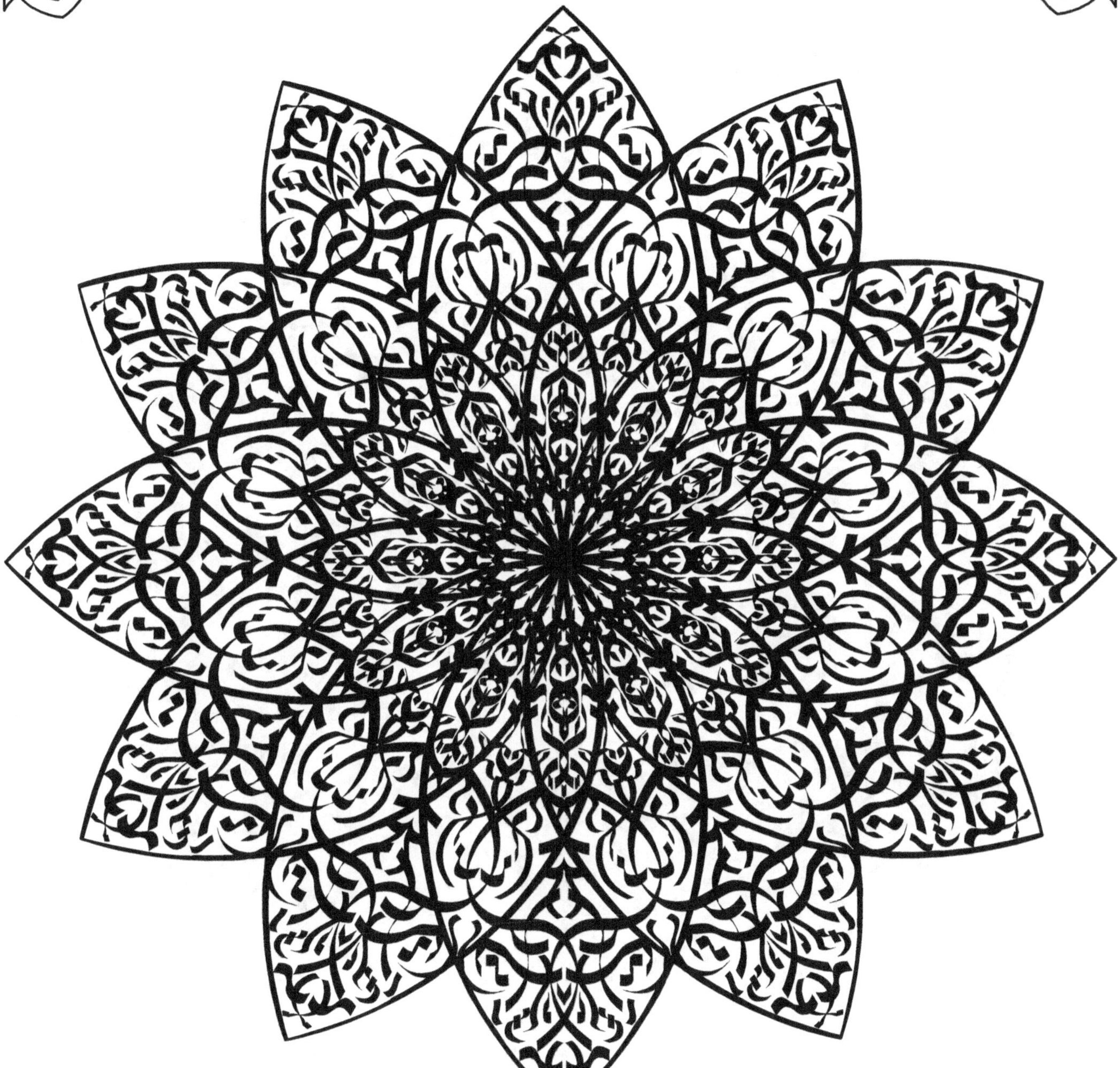

Abo Alaa

INTERNATIONAL DESIGNERDD

# Abo Alaa

INTERNATIONAL DESIGNERDD

# Mama mandala

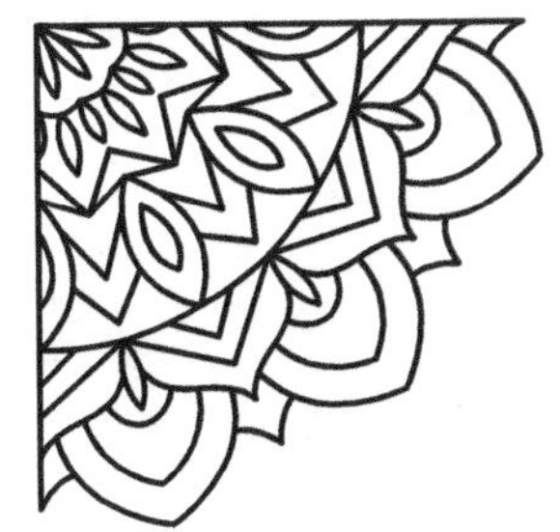
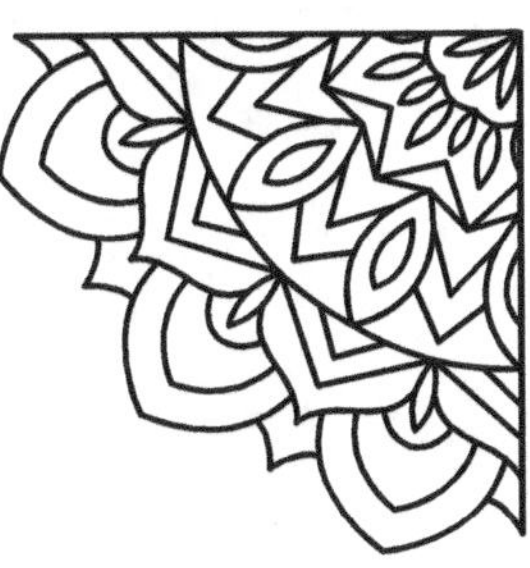
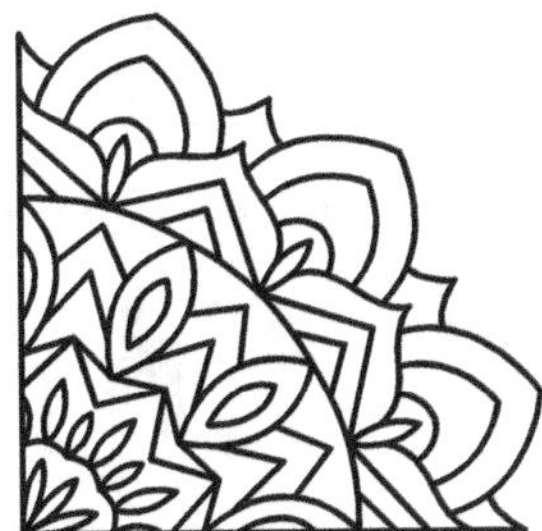

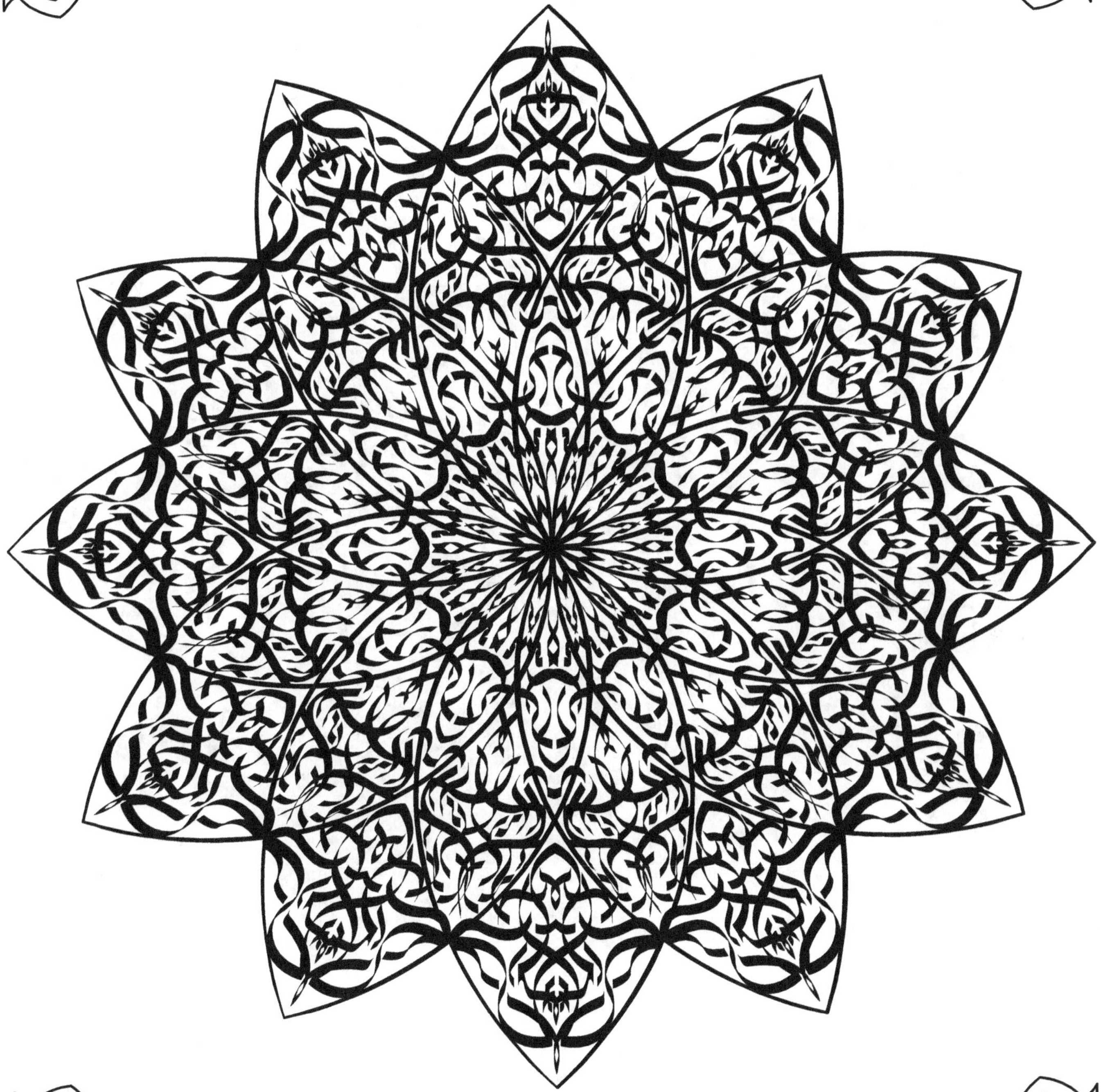

Abo Alaa

INTERNATIONAL DESIGNERDD

# Abo Alaa

INTERNATIONAL DESIGNERDD

# Mama mandala

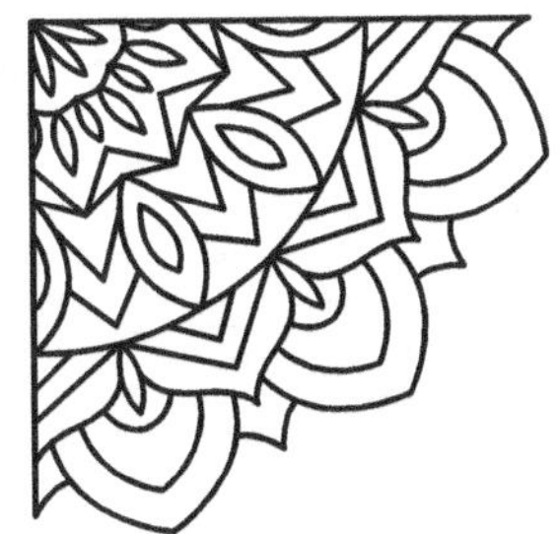

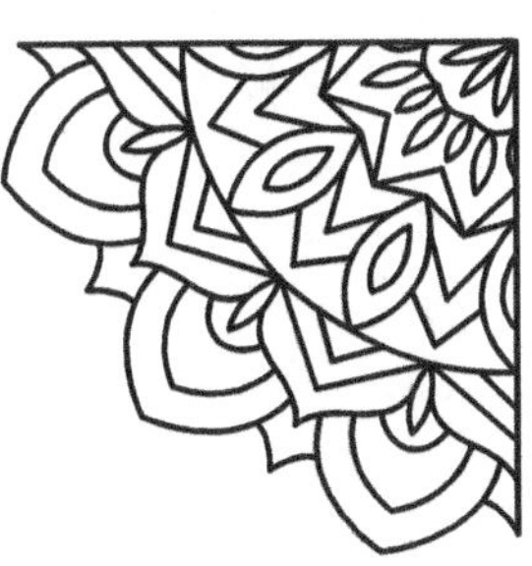

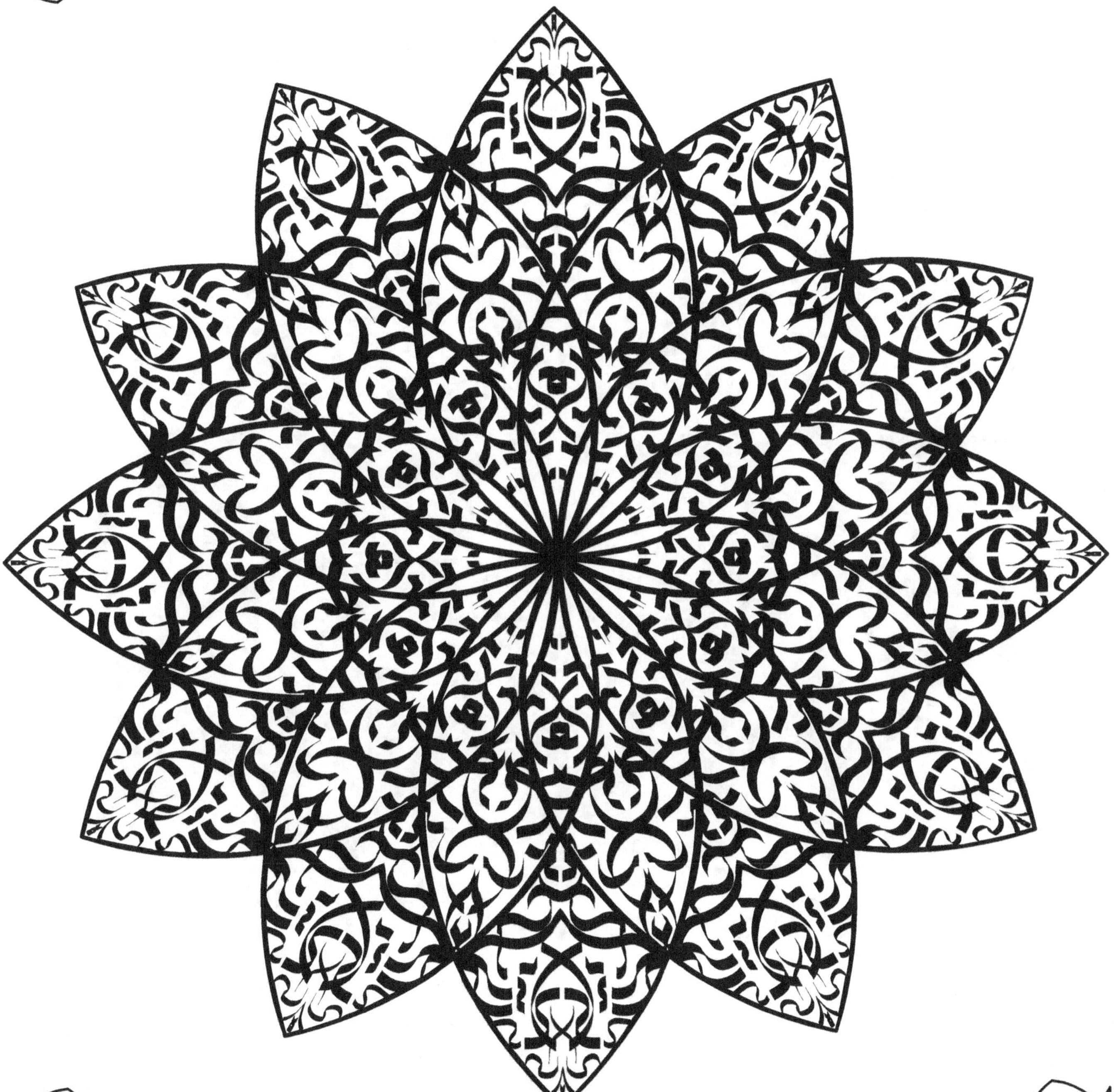

Abo Alaa

INTERNATIONAL DESIGNERDD

# Abo Alaa

INTERNATIONAL DESIGNERDD

# Mama mandala

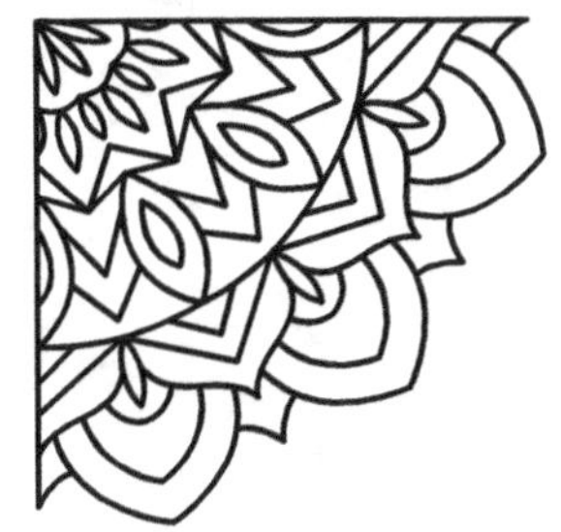
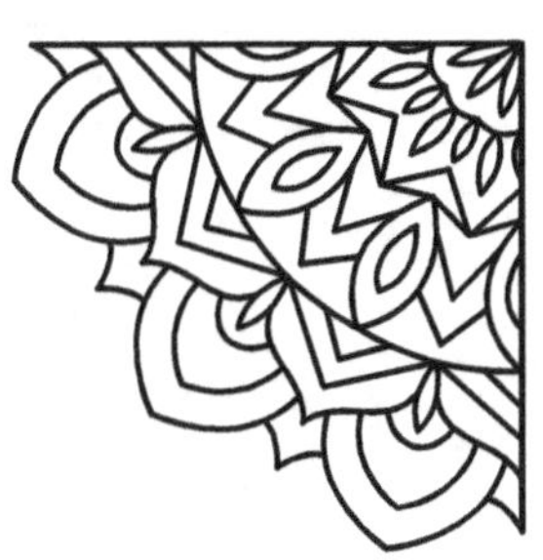

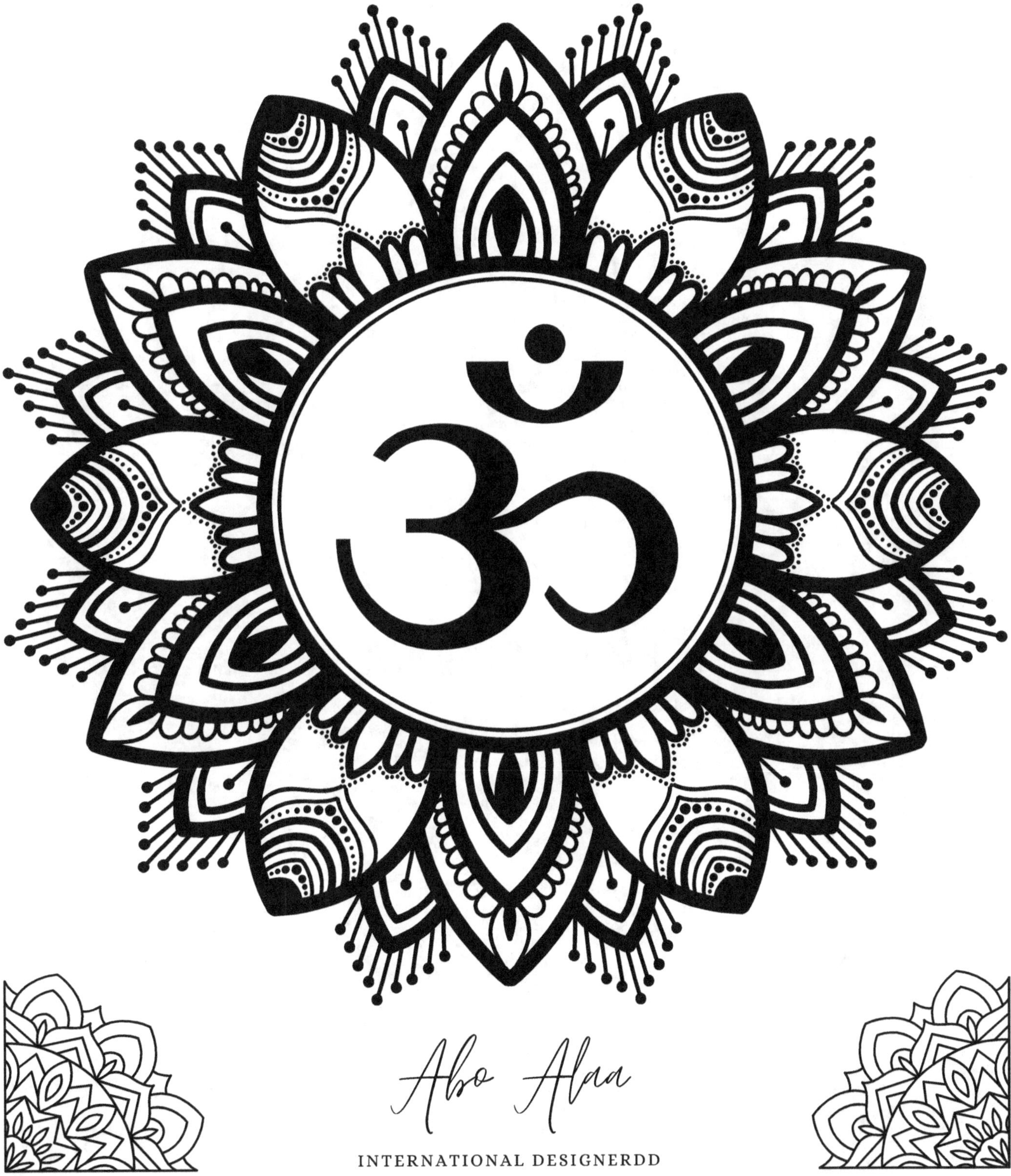

Abo Alaa

INTERNATIONAL DESIGNERDD

*Abo Alaa*

INTERNATIONAL DESIGNERDD

# Mama mandala

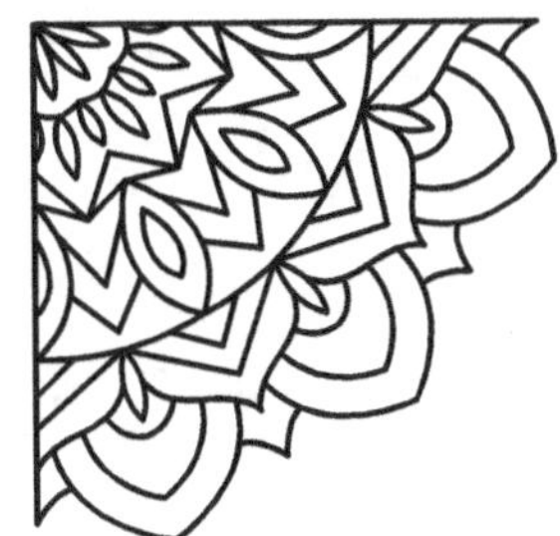
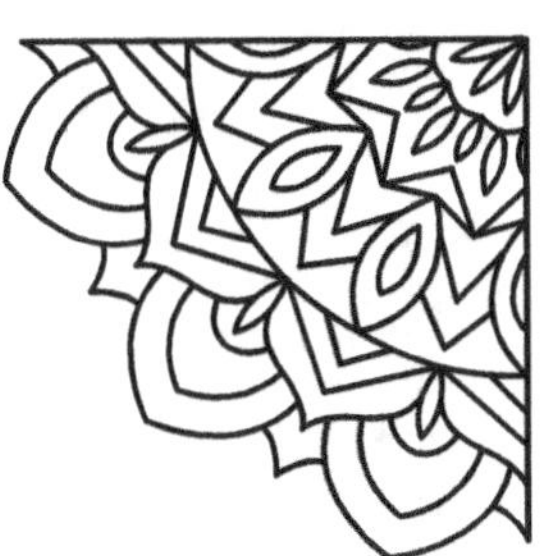

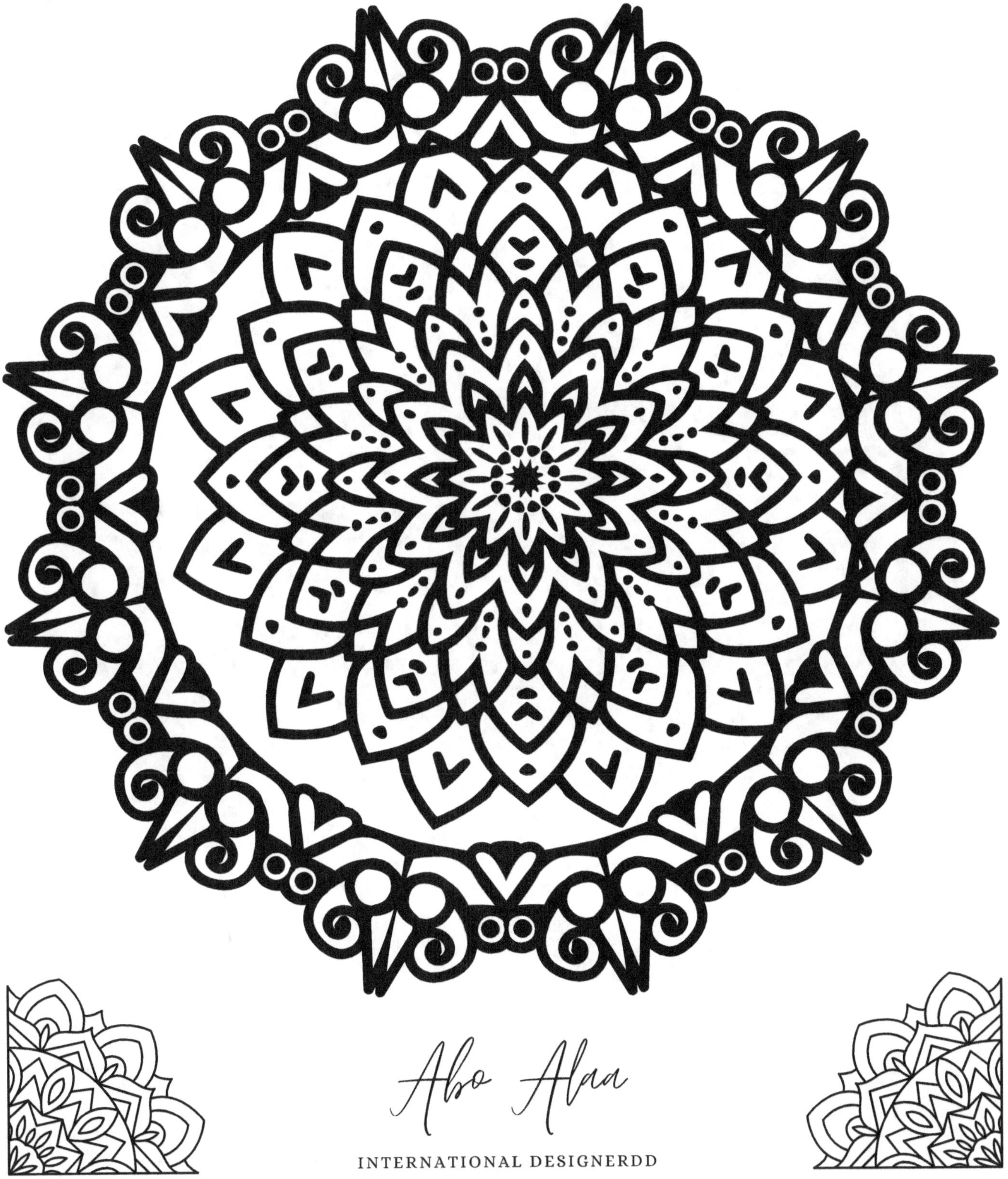

Abo Alaa

INTERNATIONAL DESIGNERDD

# Abo Alaa

INTERNATIONAL DESIGNERDD

# Mama mandala

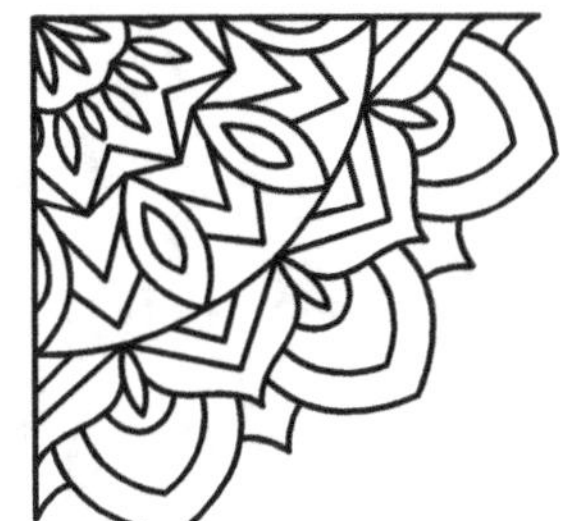
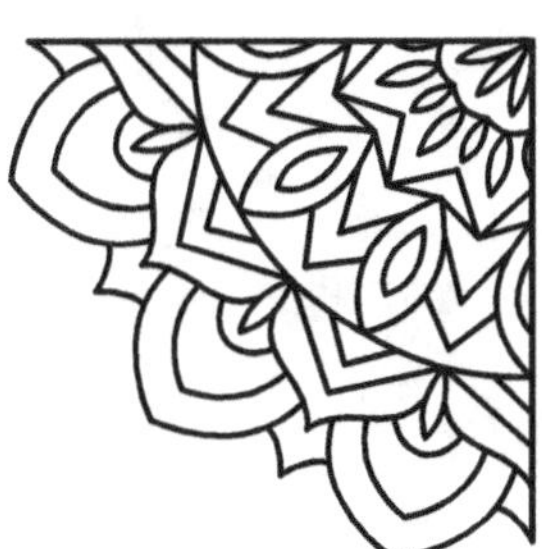
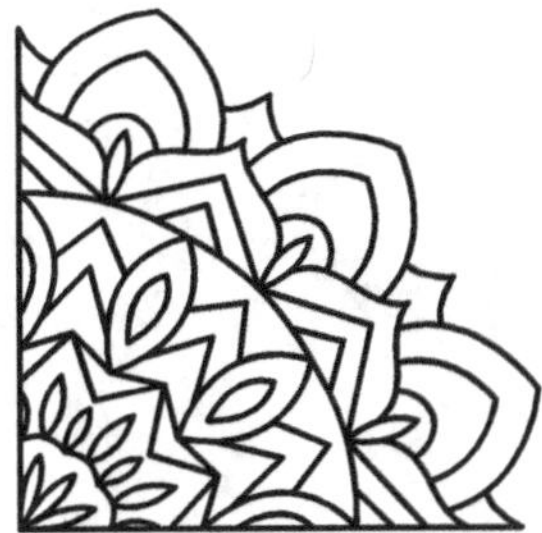

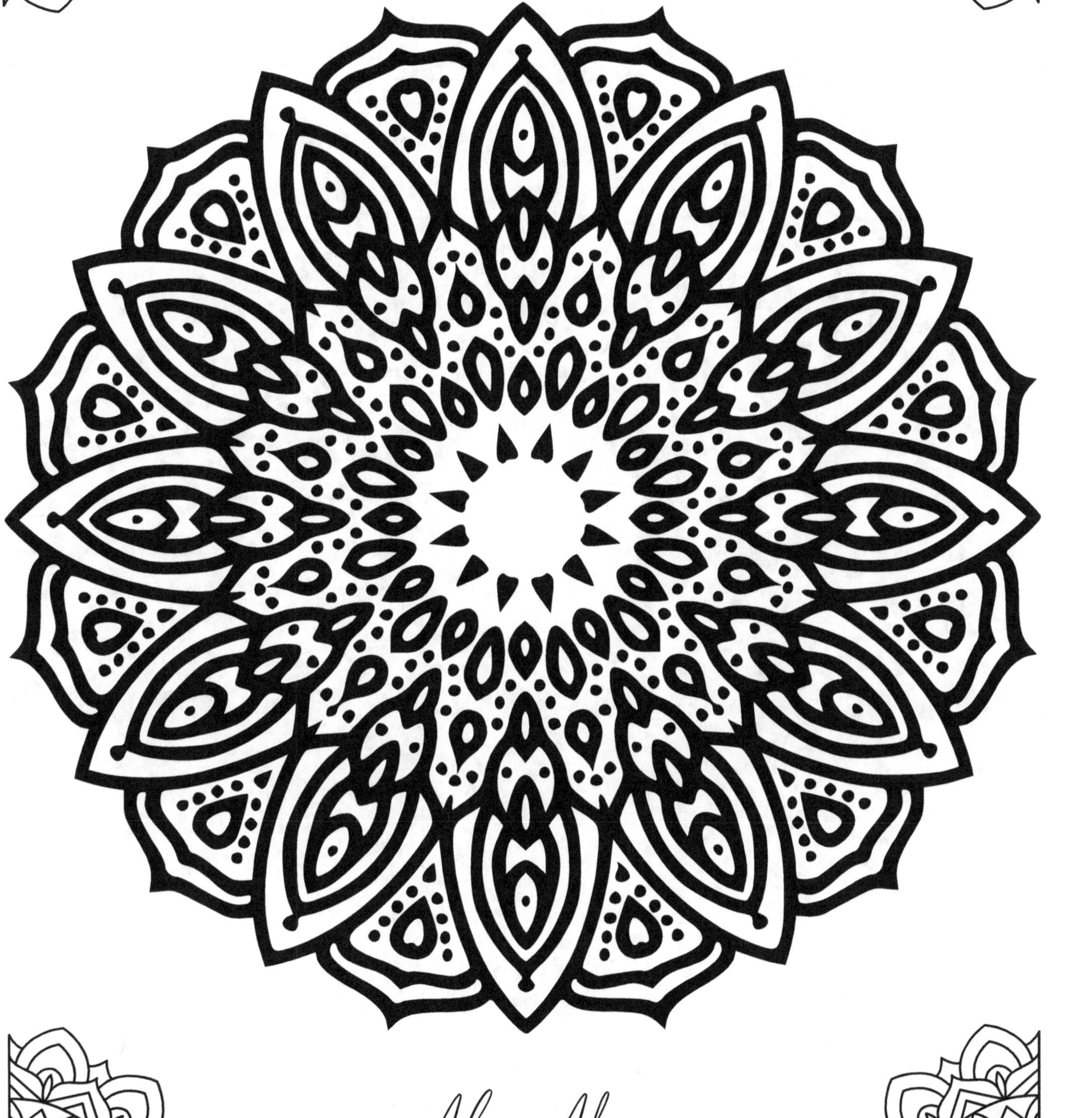

Abo Alaa

INTERNATIONAL DESIGNERDD

# Abo Alaa

INTERNATIONAL DESIGNERDD

# Mama mandala

# Abo Alaa

INTERNATIONAL DESIGNERDD

# Mama mandala

# Abo Alaa

INTERNATIONAL DESIGNERDD

# Mama mandala

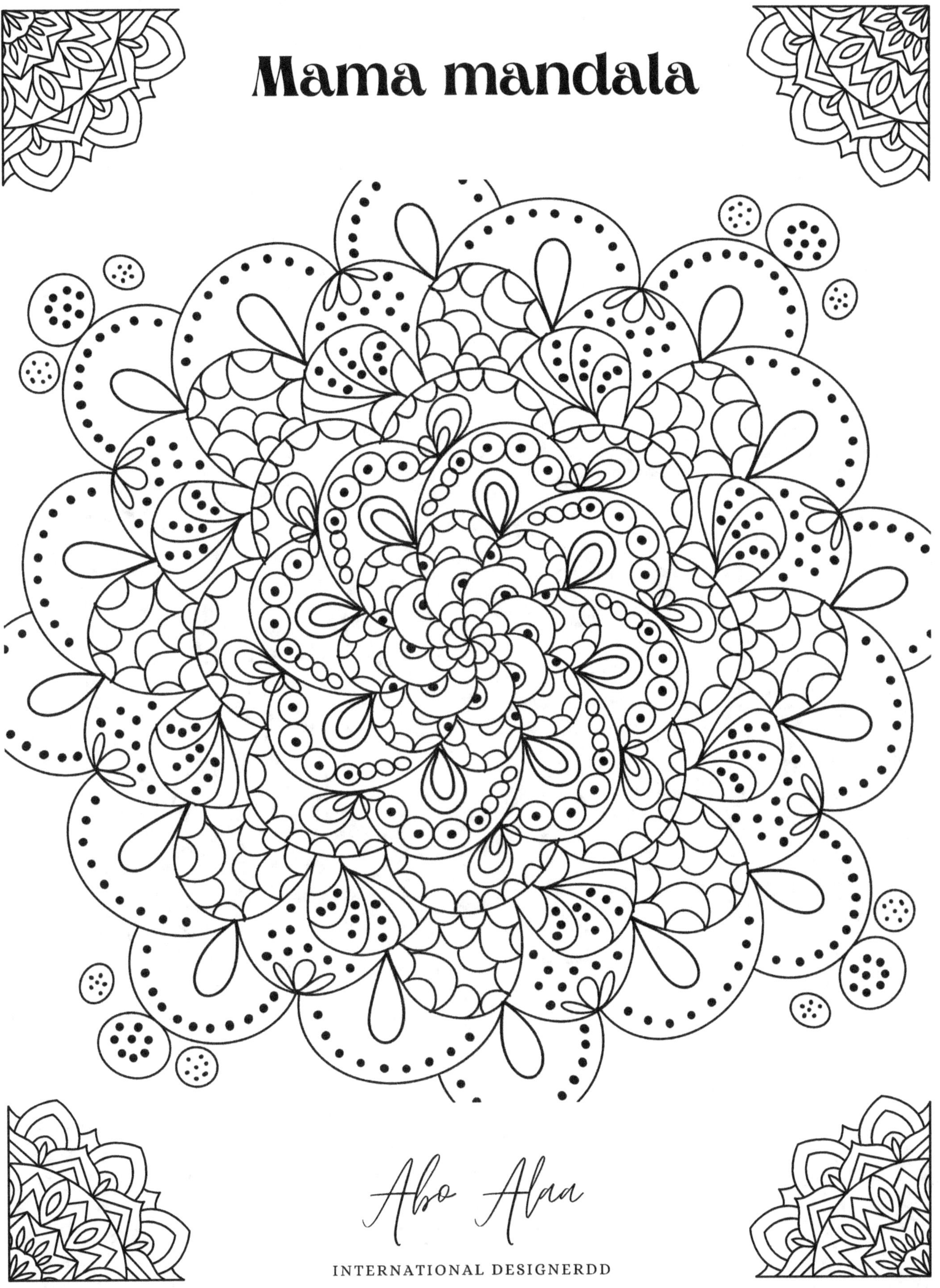

Abo Alaa

INTERNATIONAL DESIGNERDD

# Mama mandala

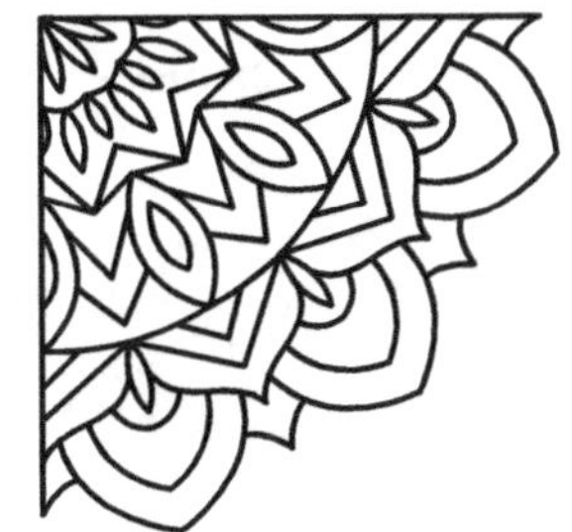
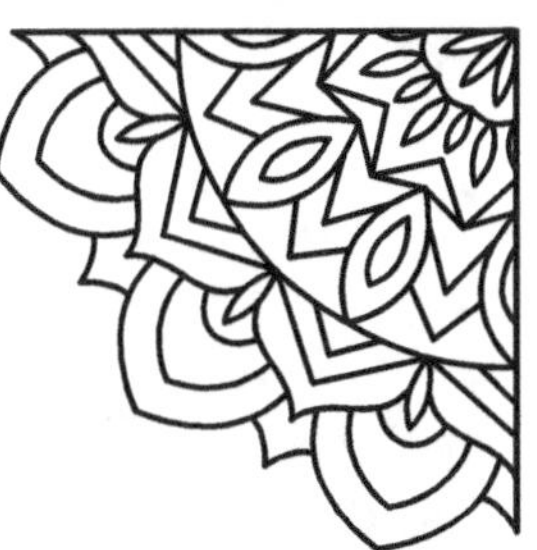
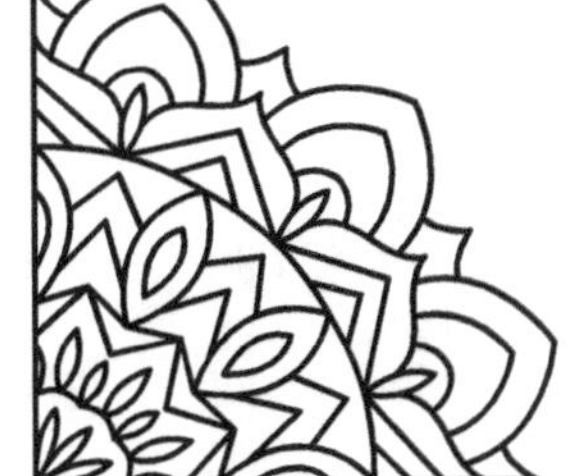

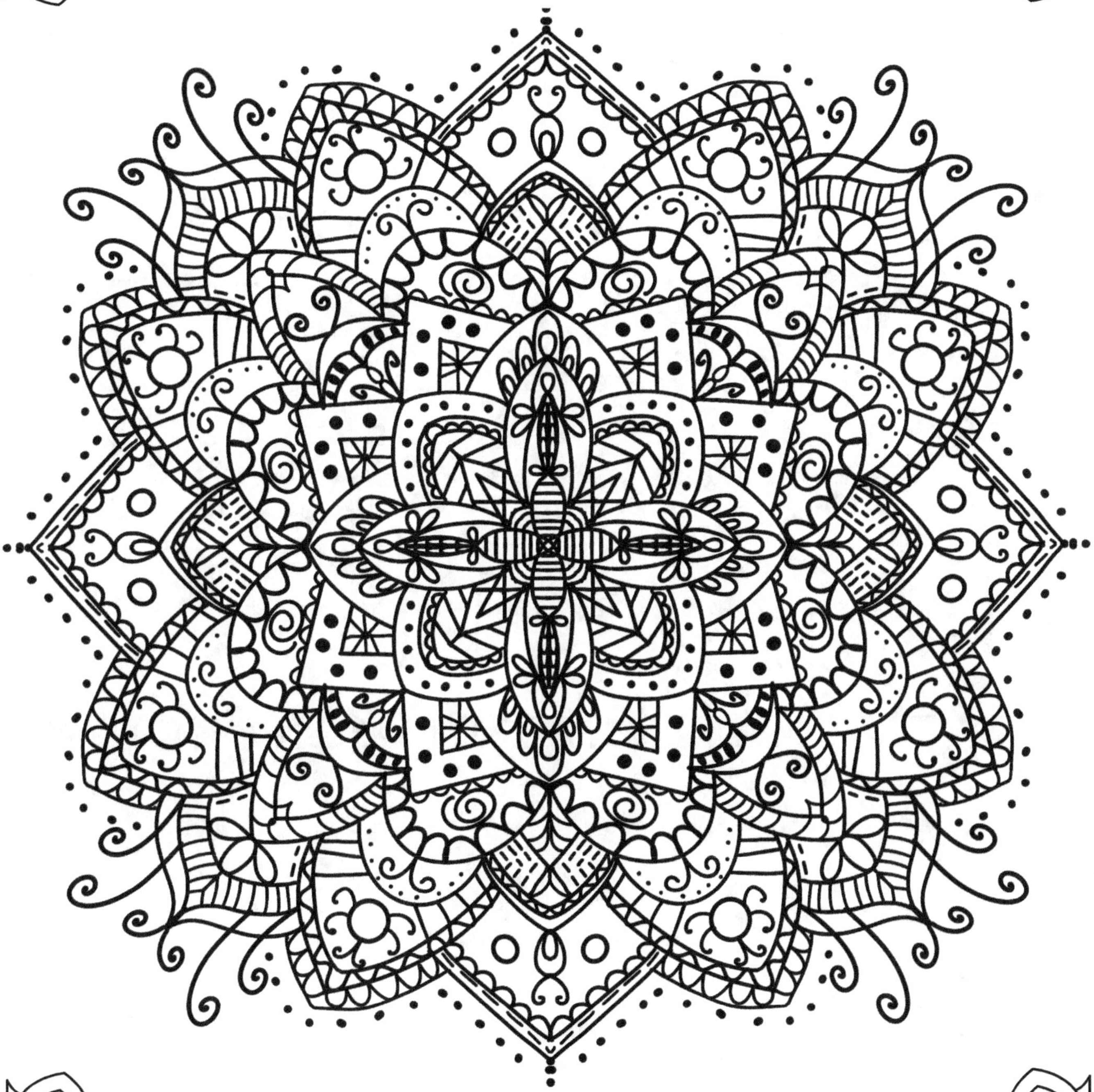

*Abo Alaa*

INTERNATIONAL DESIGNERDD

# Abo Alaa

INTERNATIONAL DESIGNERDD

# Mama mandala

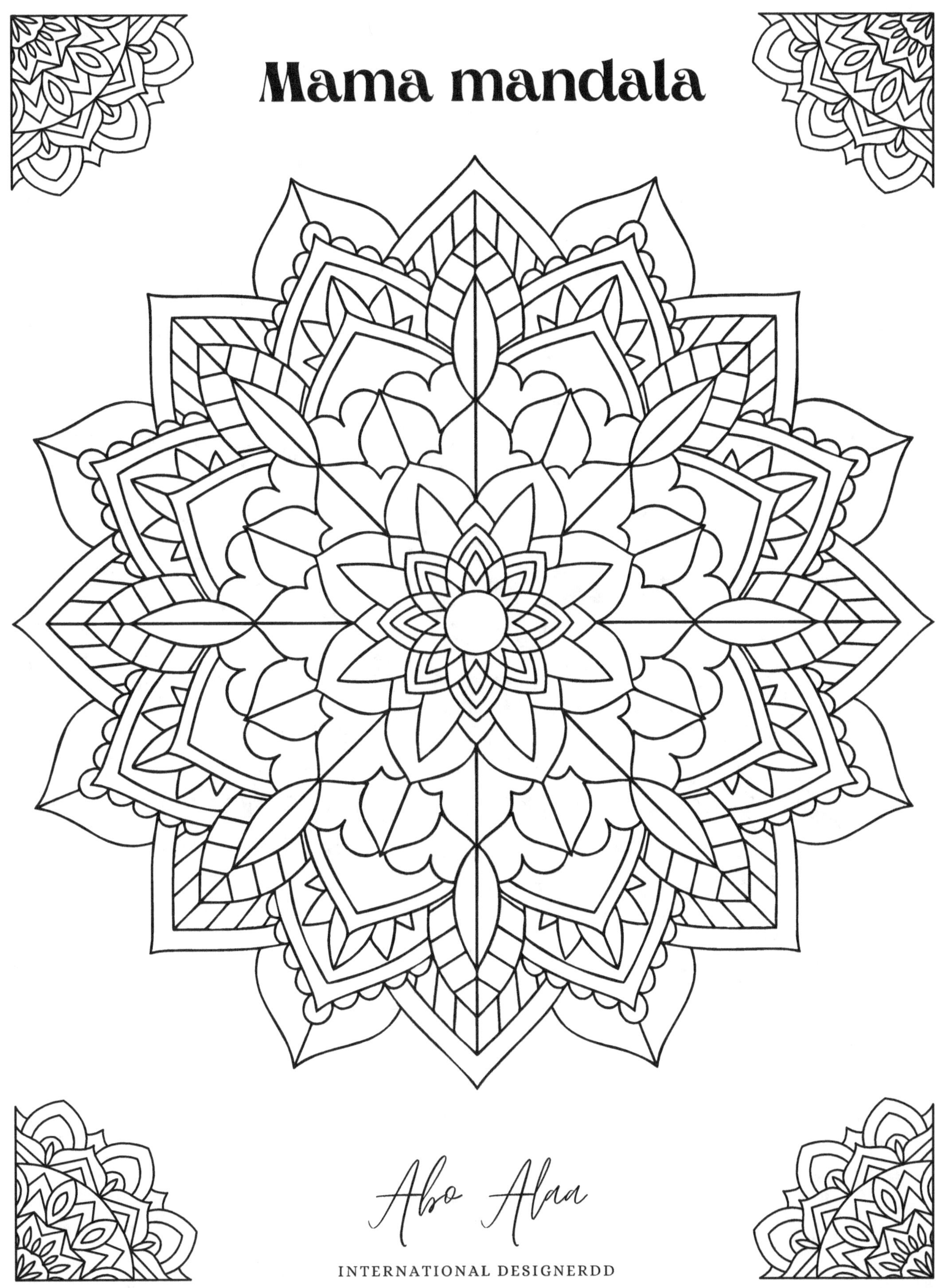

Abo Alaa

INTERNATIONAL DESIGNERDD

# Abo Alaa

INTERNATIONAL DESIGNERDD

# Mama mandala

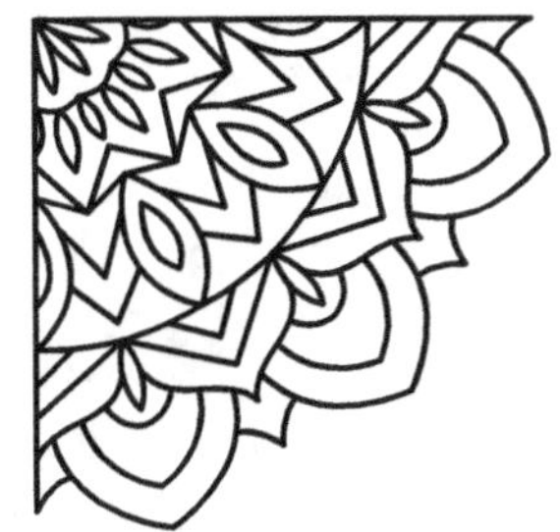
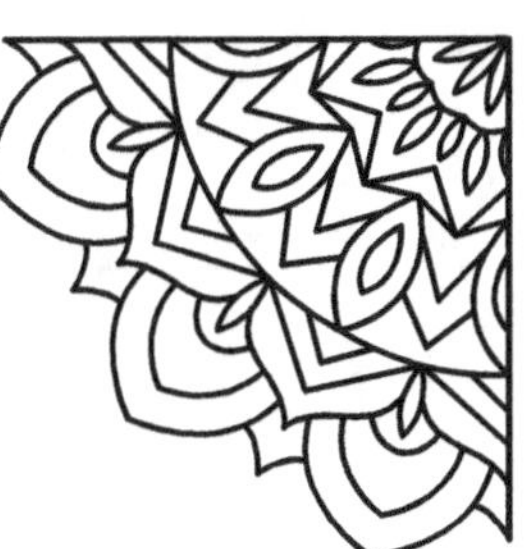
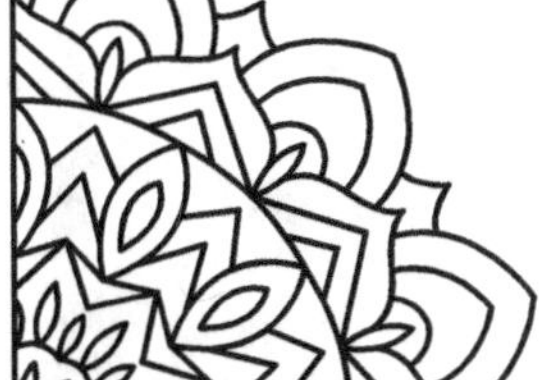

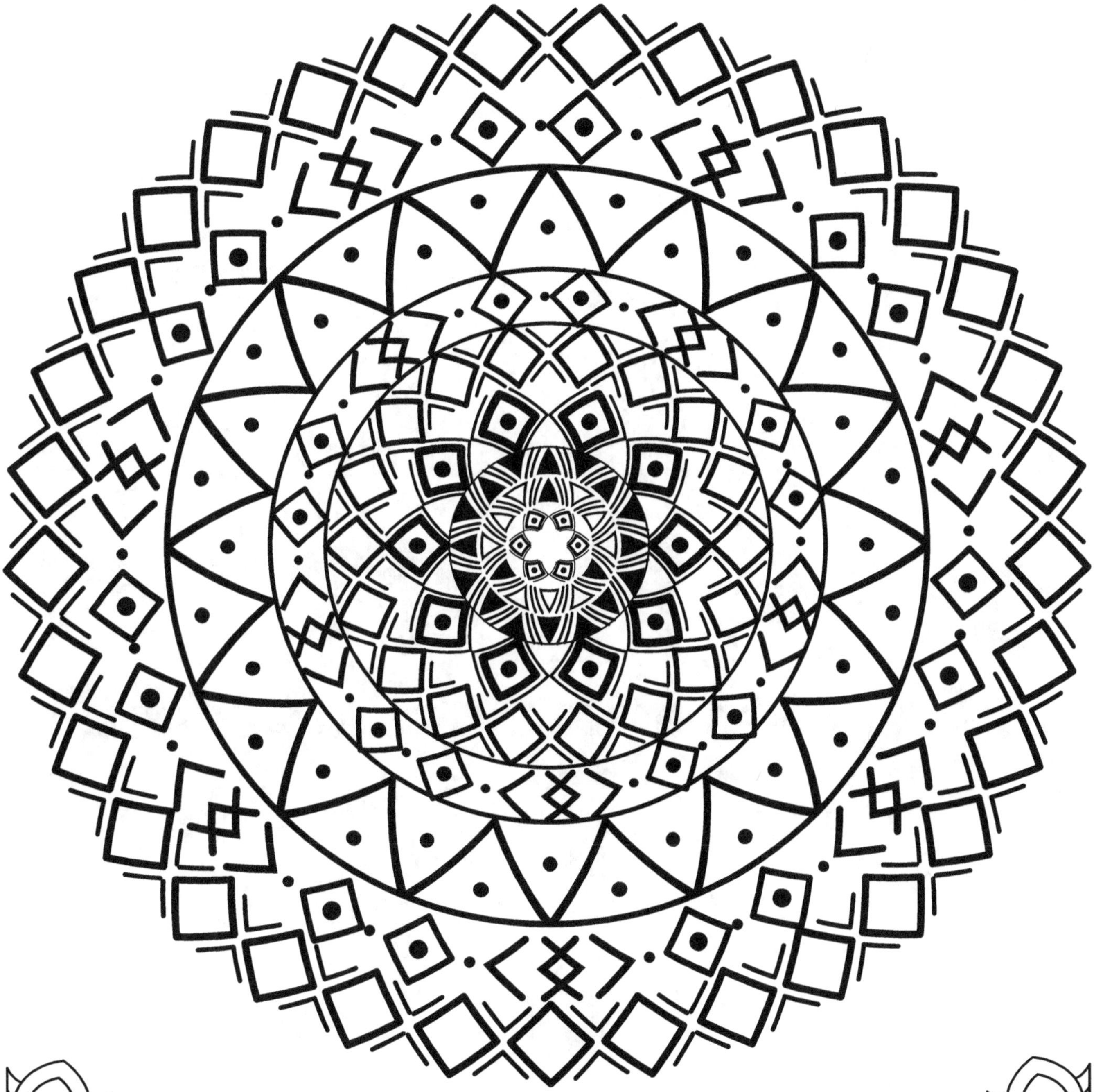

*Abo Alaa*

INTERNATIONAL DESIGNERDD

Abo Alaa
INTERNATIONAL DESIGNERDD

# Mama mandala

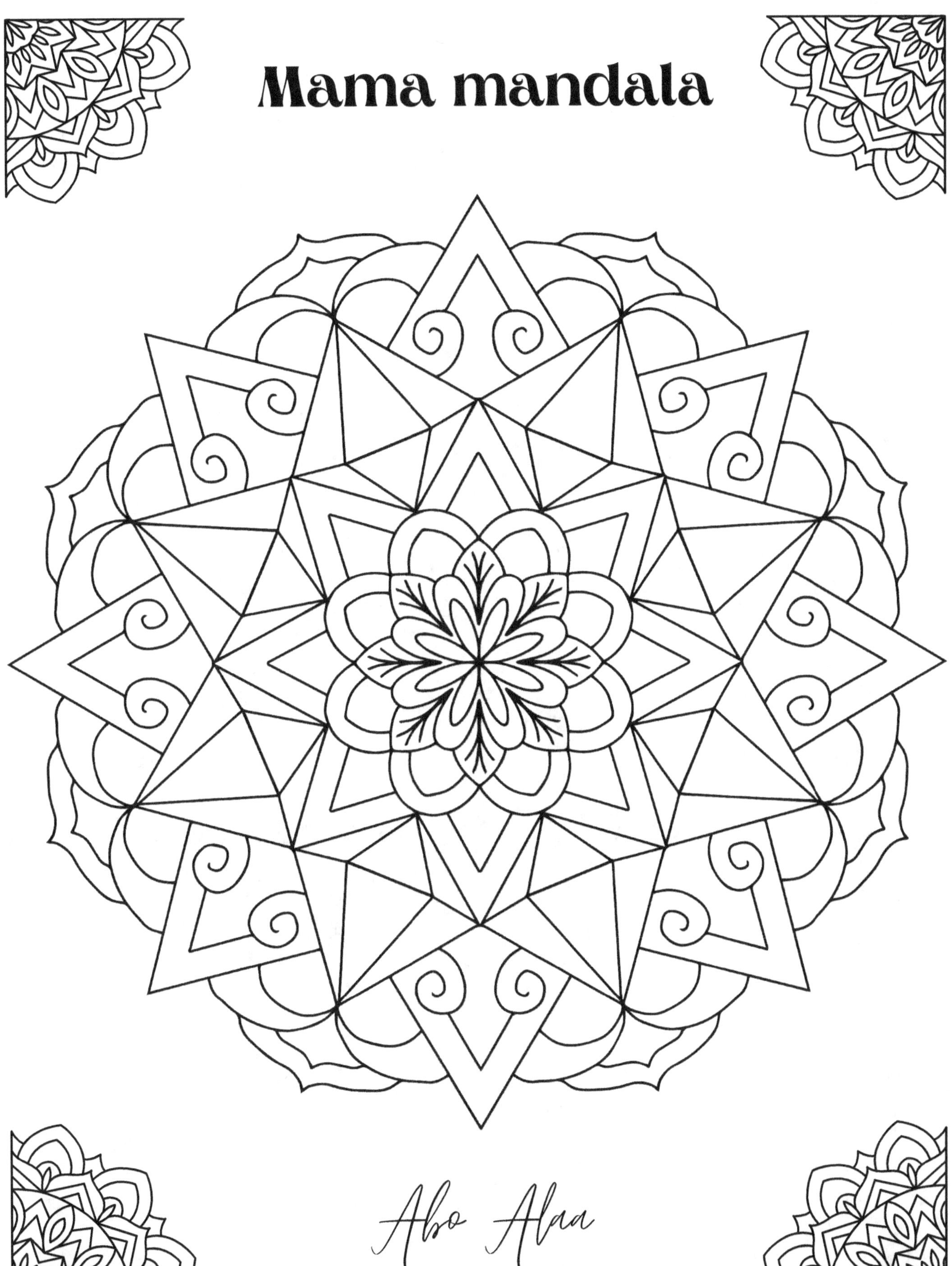

Abo Alaa

INTERNATIONAL DESIGNERDD

# Abo Alaa

INTERNATIONAL DESIGNERDD

# Mama mandala

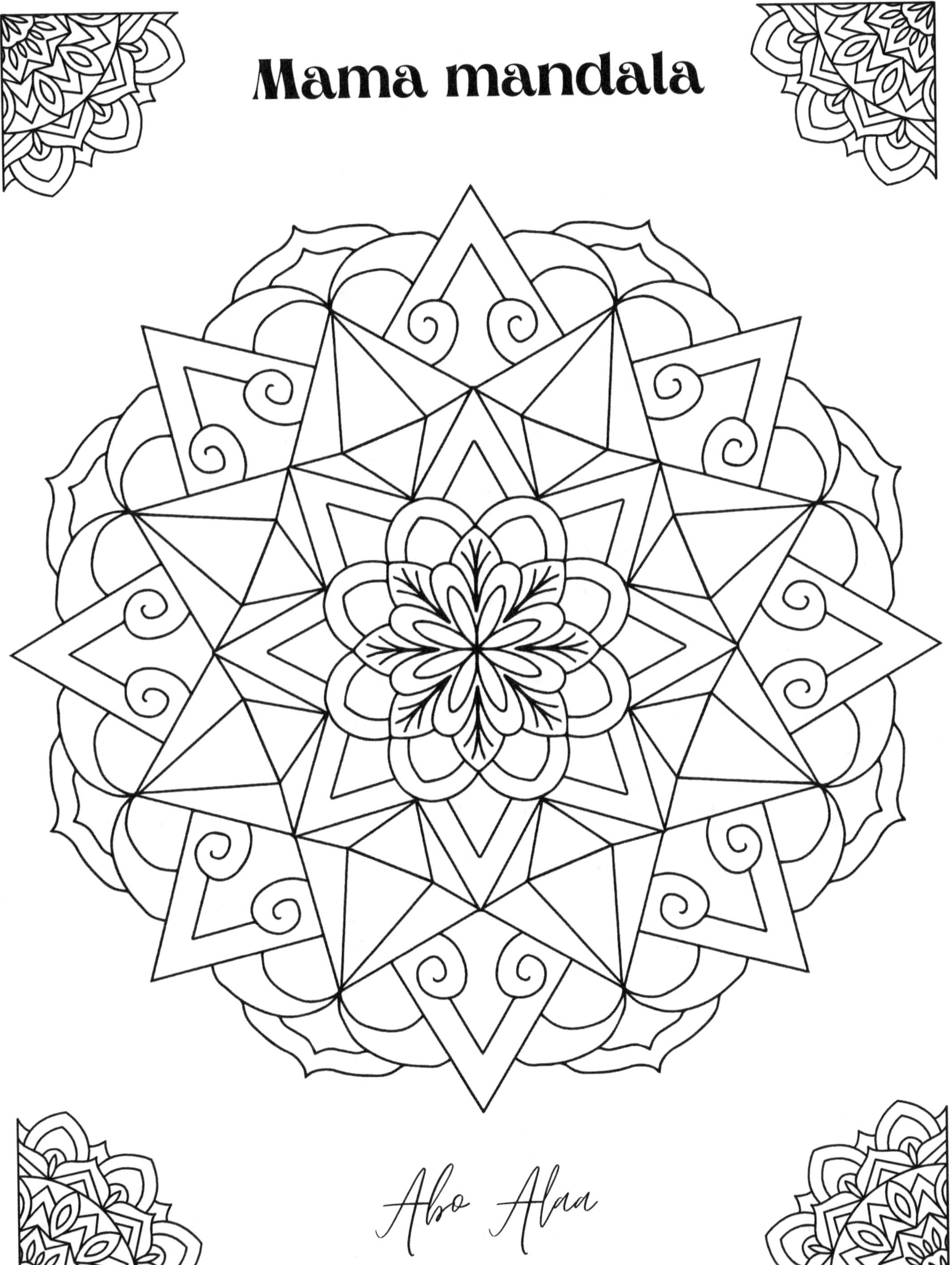

Abo Alaa

INTERNATIONAL DESIGNERDD

Abo Alaa

INTERNATIONAL DESIGNERDD

# Mama mandala

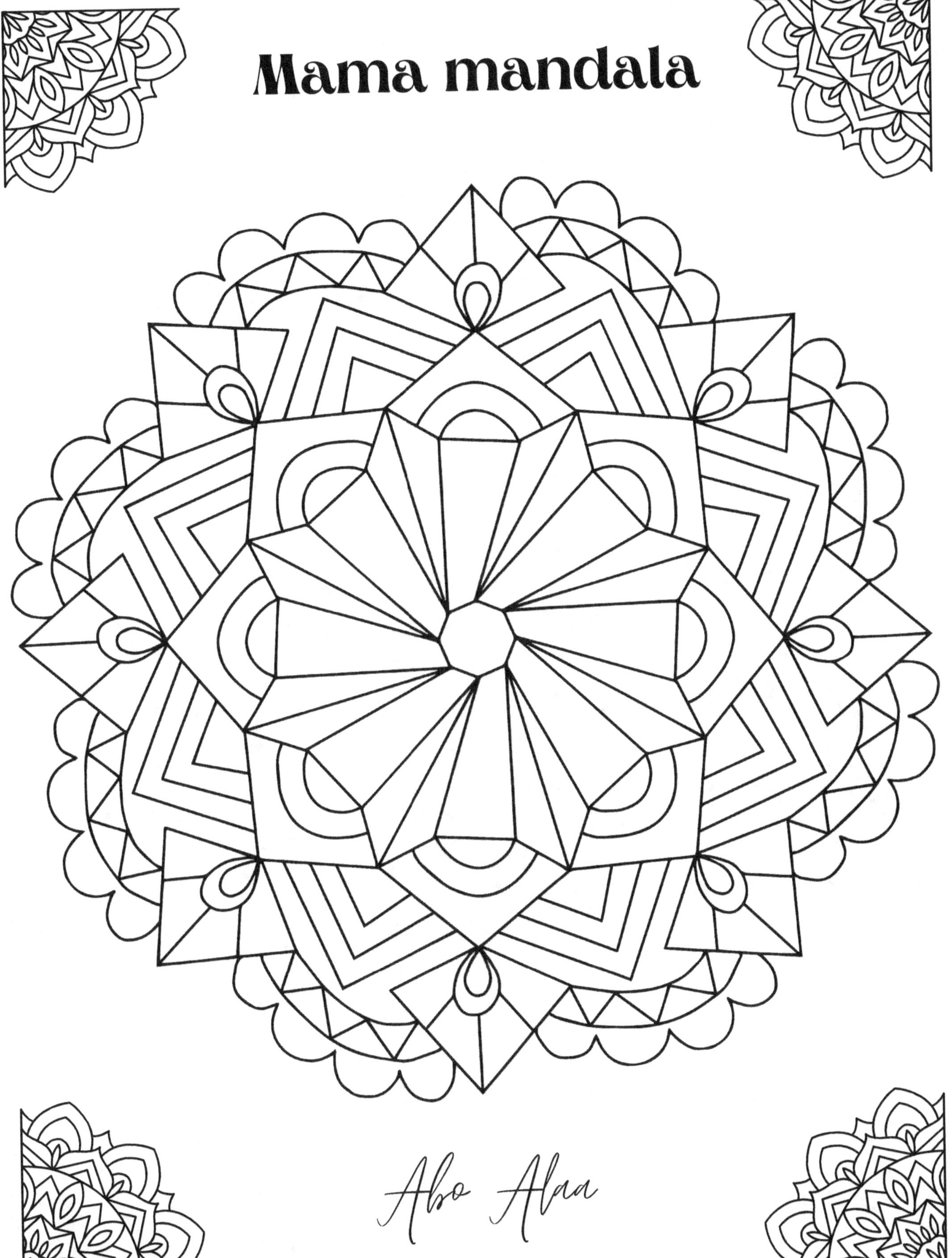

# Abo Alaa

INTERNATIONAL DESIGNERDD

# Mama mandala

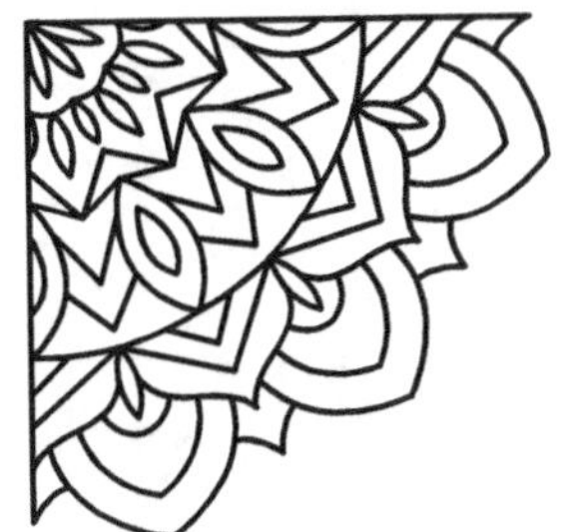
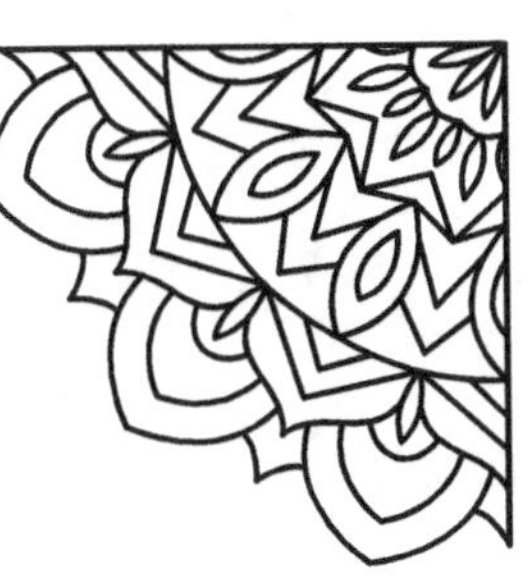
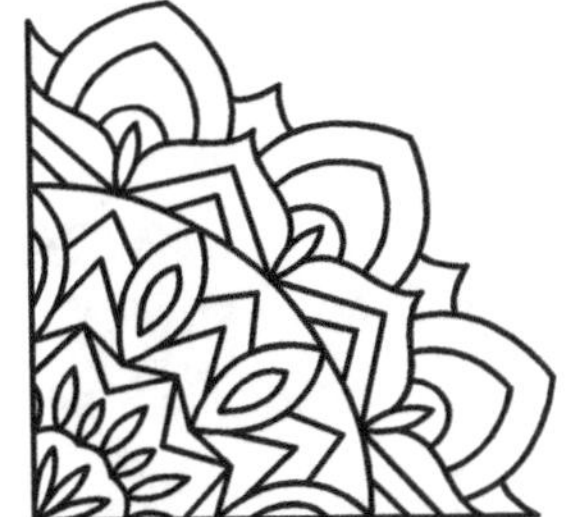
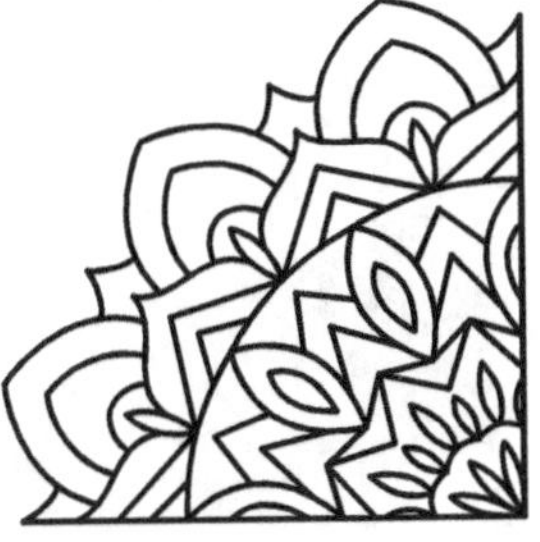

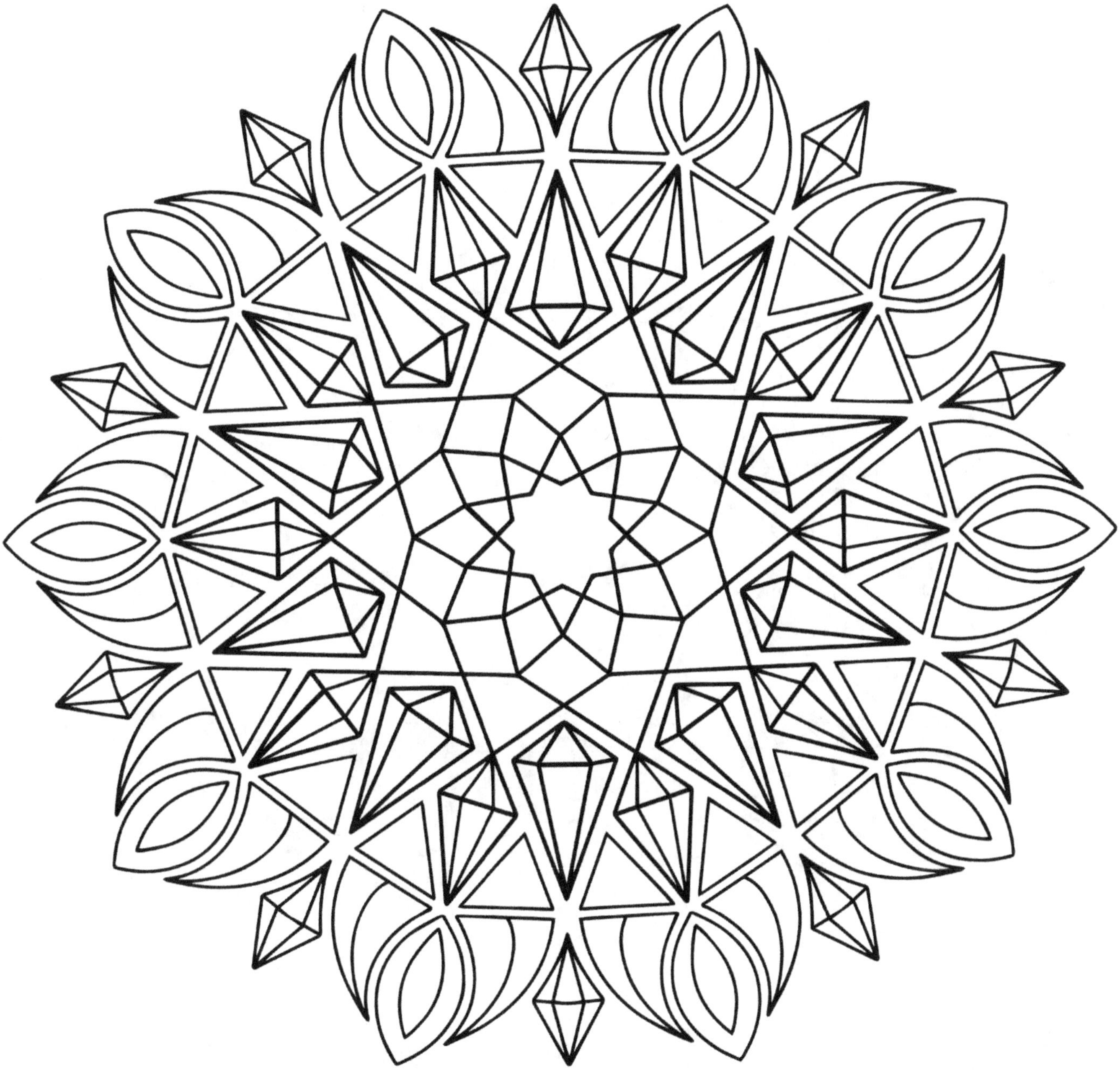

Abo Alaa

INTERNATIONAL DESIGNERDD

# Abo Alaa

INTERNATIONAL DESIGNERDD

# Mama mandala

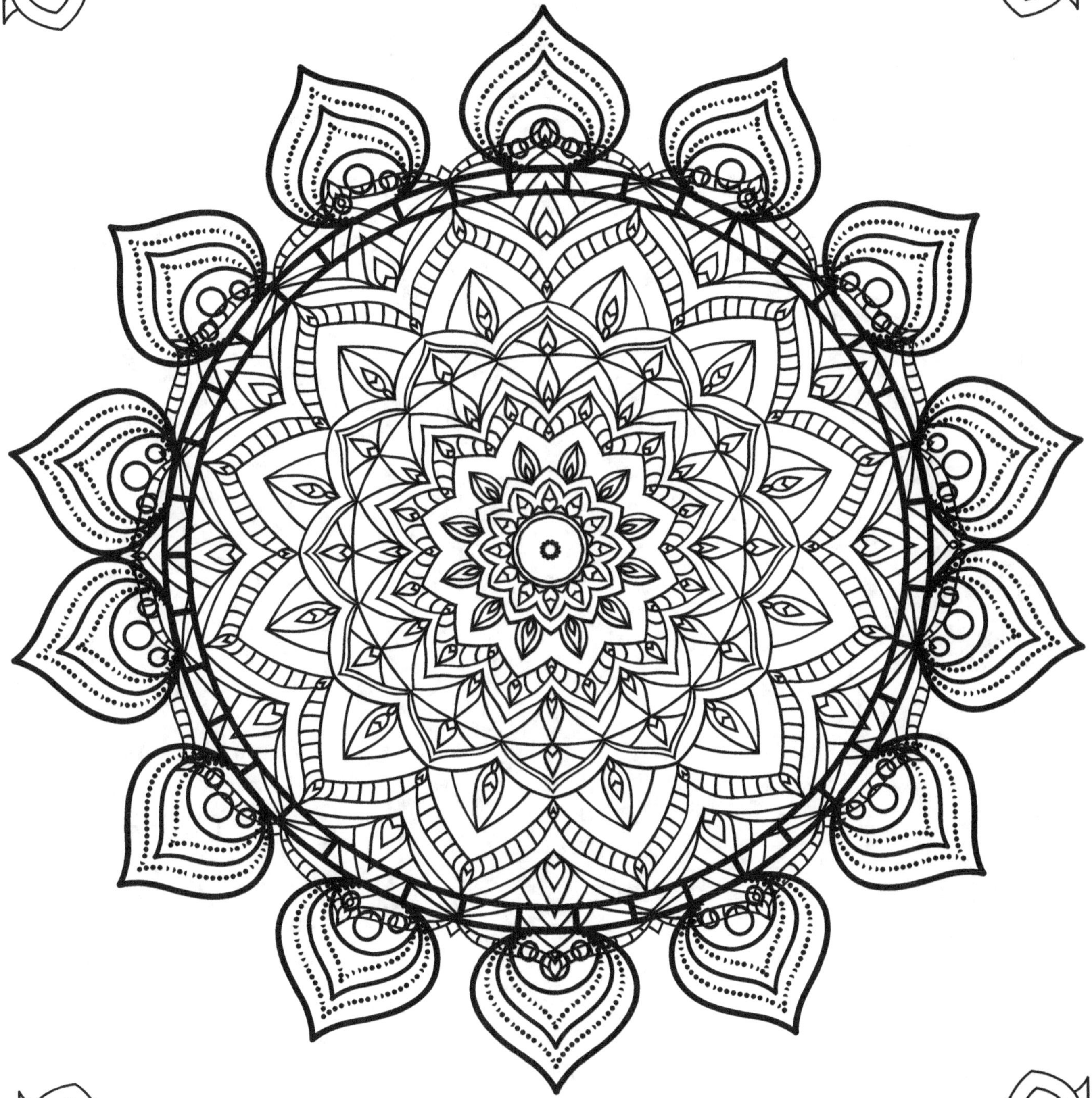

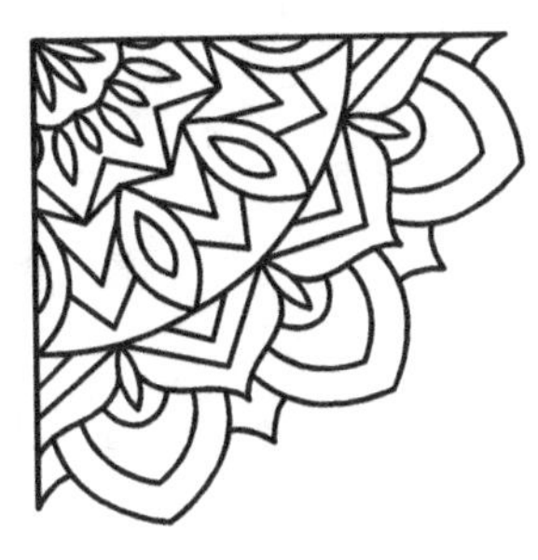
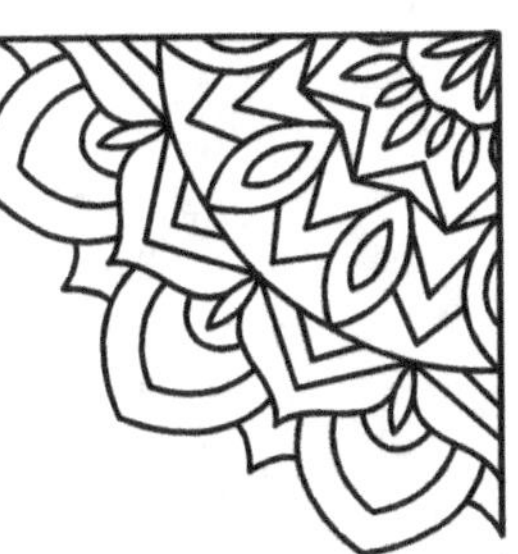
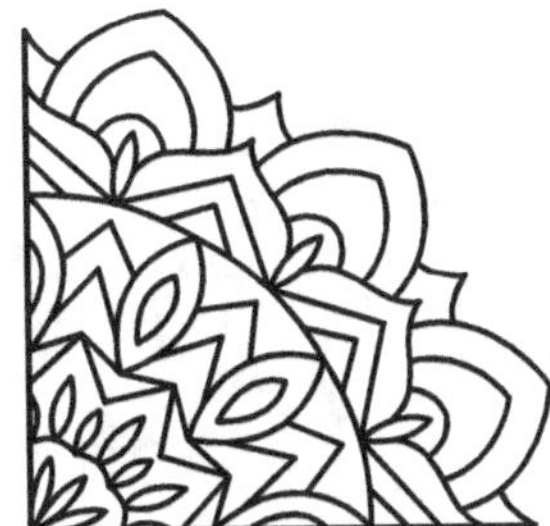

*Abo Alaa*

INTERNATIONAL DESIGNERDD

# Mama mandala

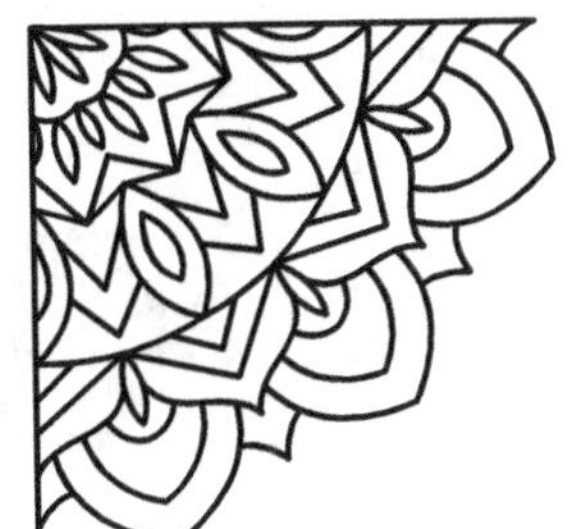
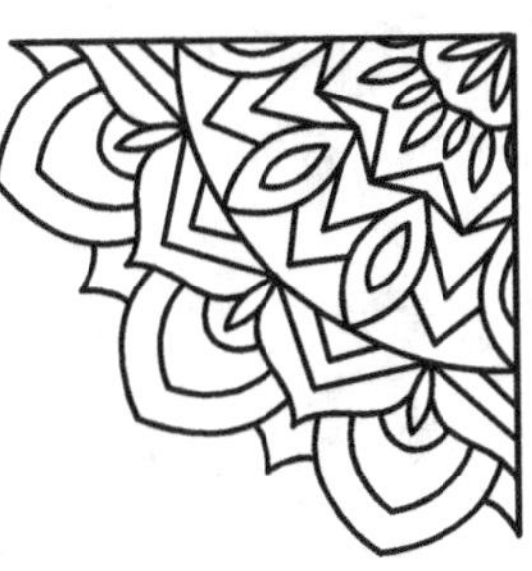
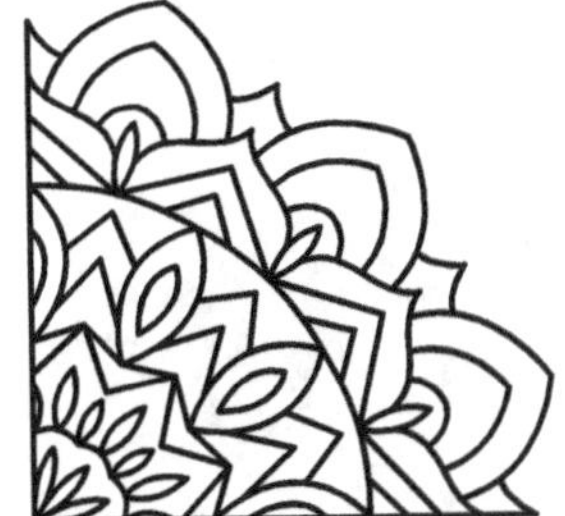

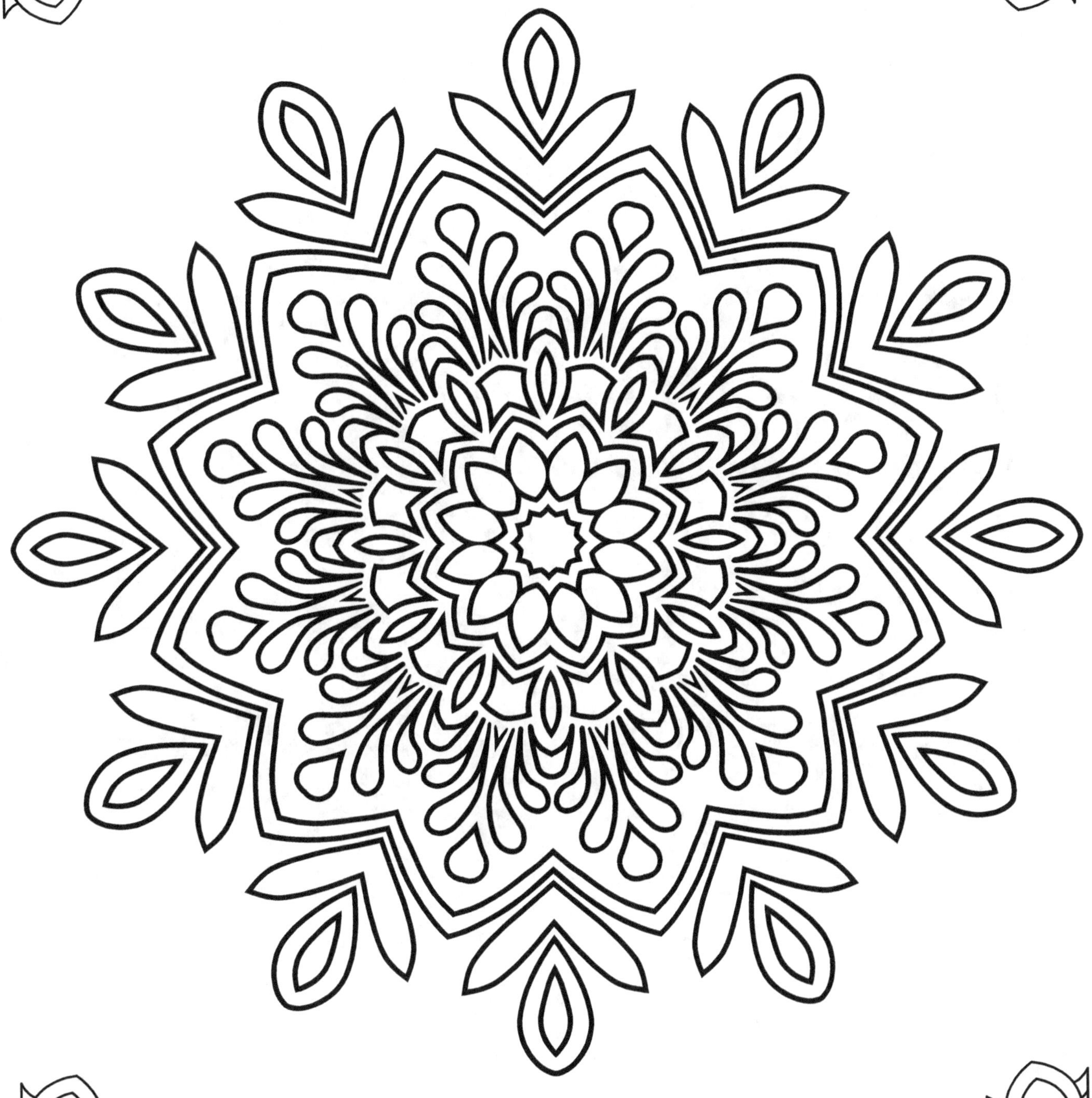

Abo Alaa

INTERNATIONAL DESIGNERDD

# Abo Alaa

INTERNATIONAL DESIGNERDD

# Mama mandala

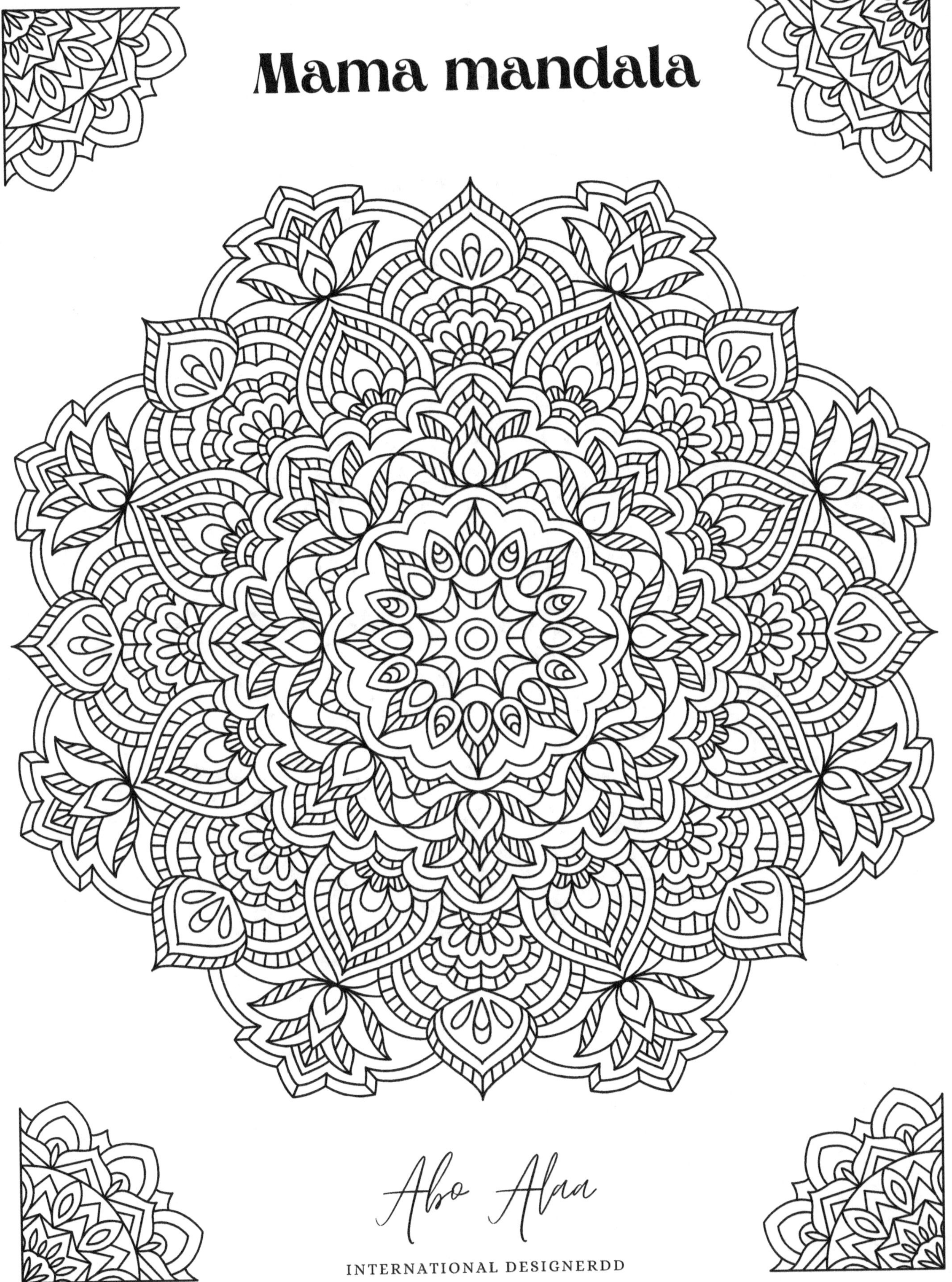

Abo Alaa

INTERNATIONAL DESIGNERDD

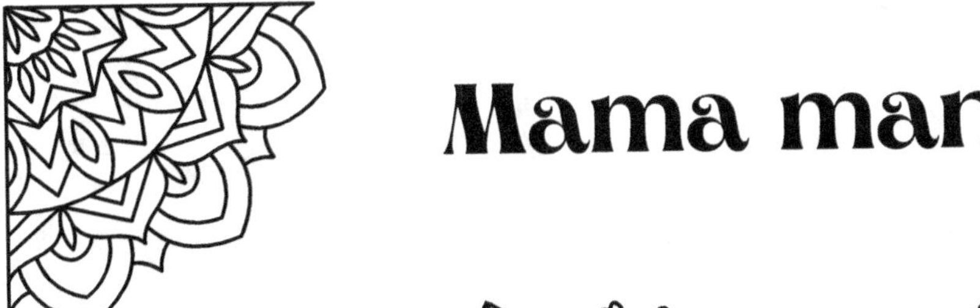

# Mama mandala

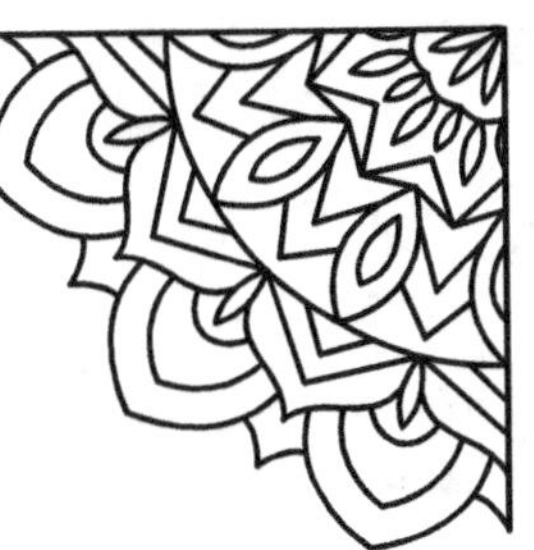

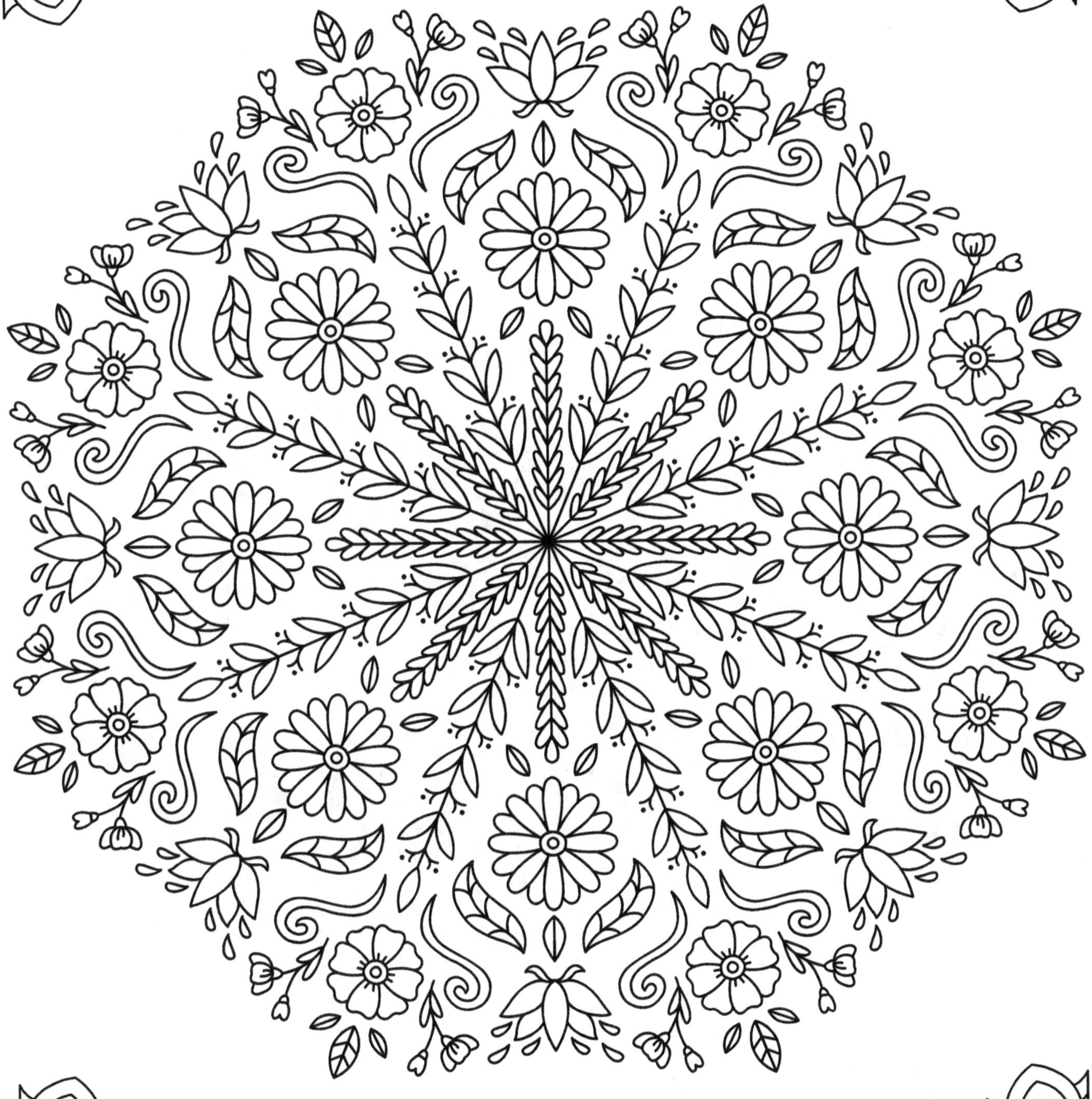

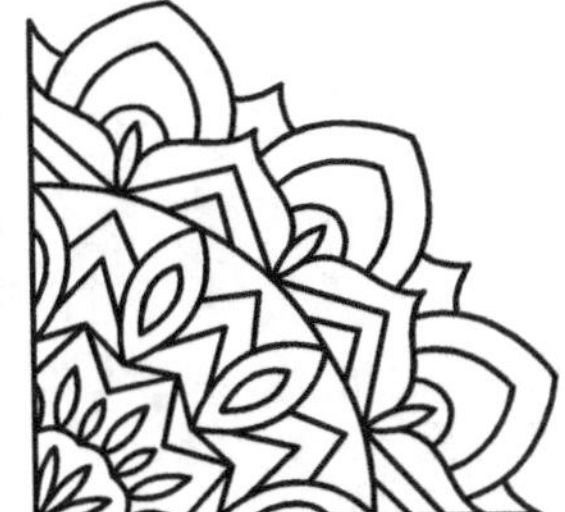

Abo Alaa

INTERNATIONAL DESIGNERDD

# INTERNATIONAL DESIGNERDD

# Mama mandala

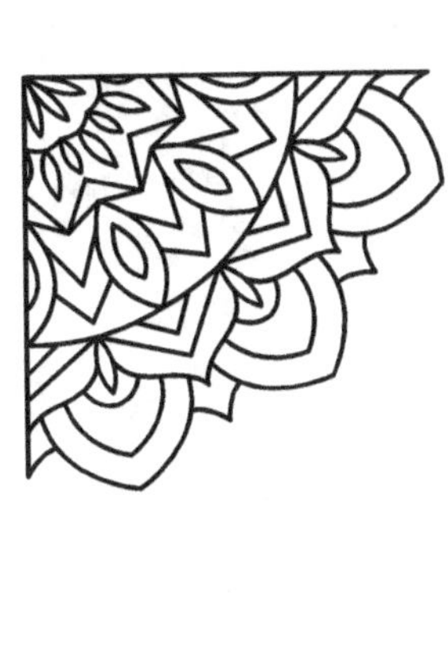

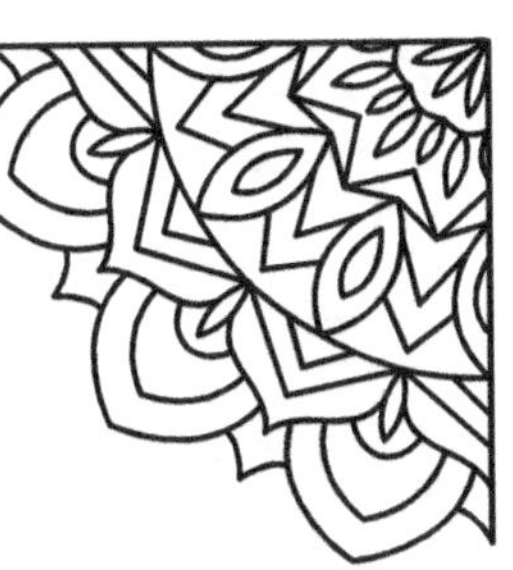

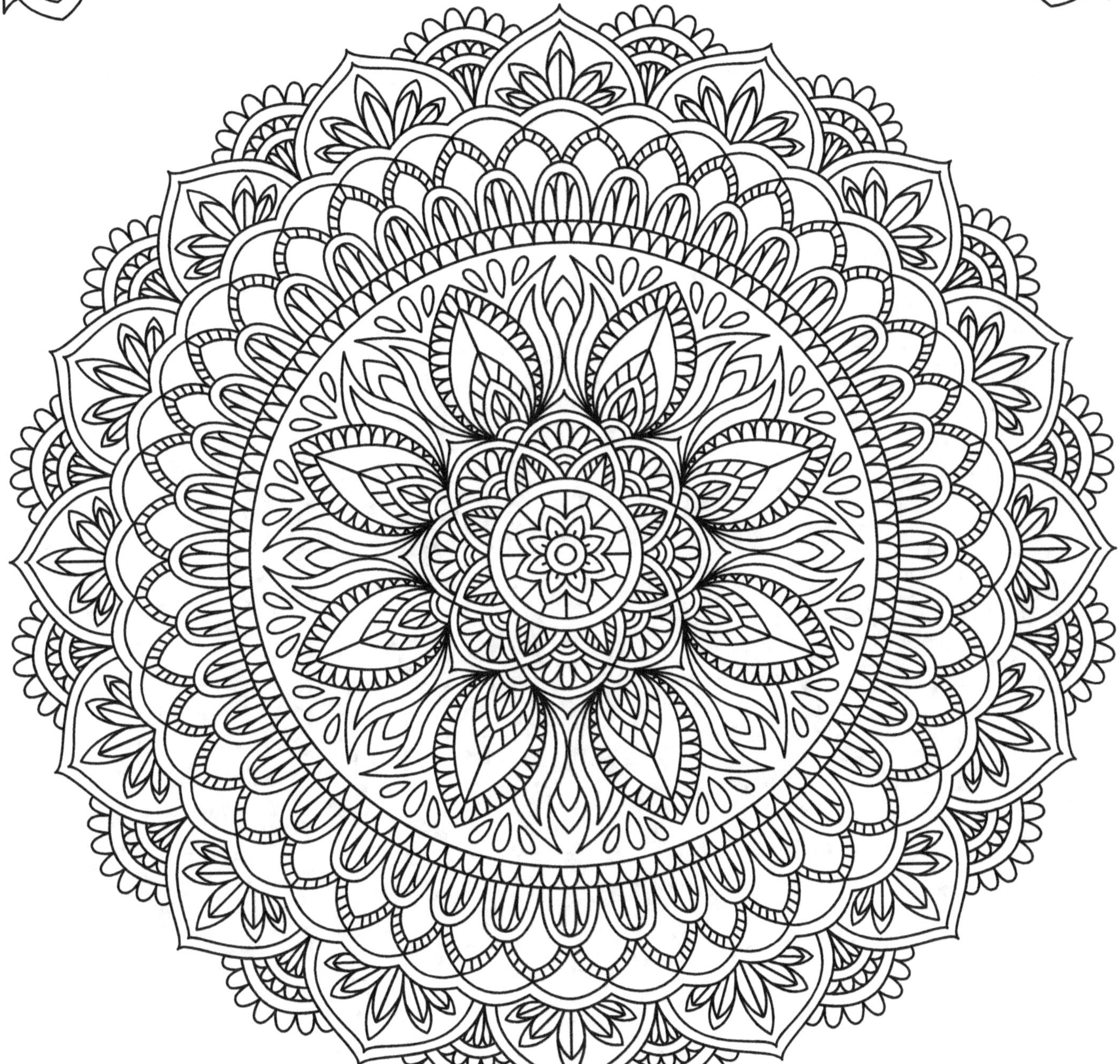

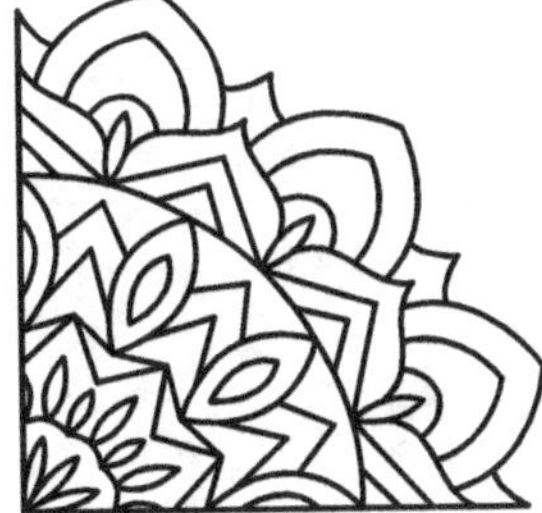

*Abo Alaa*

INTERNATIONAL DESIGNERDD

# Abo Alaa

INTERNATIONAL DESIGNERDD

# Mama mandala

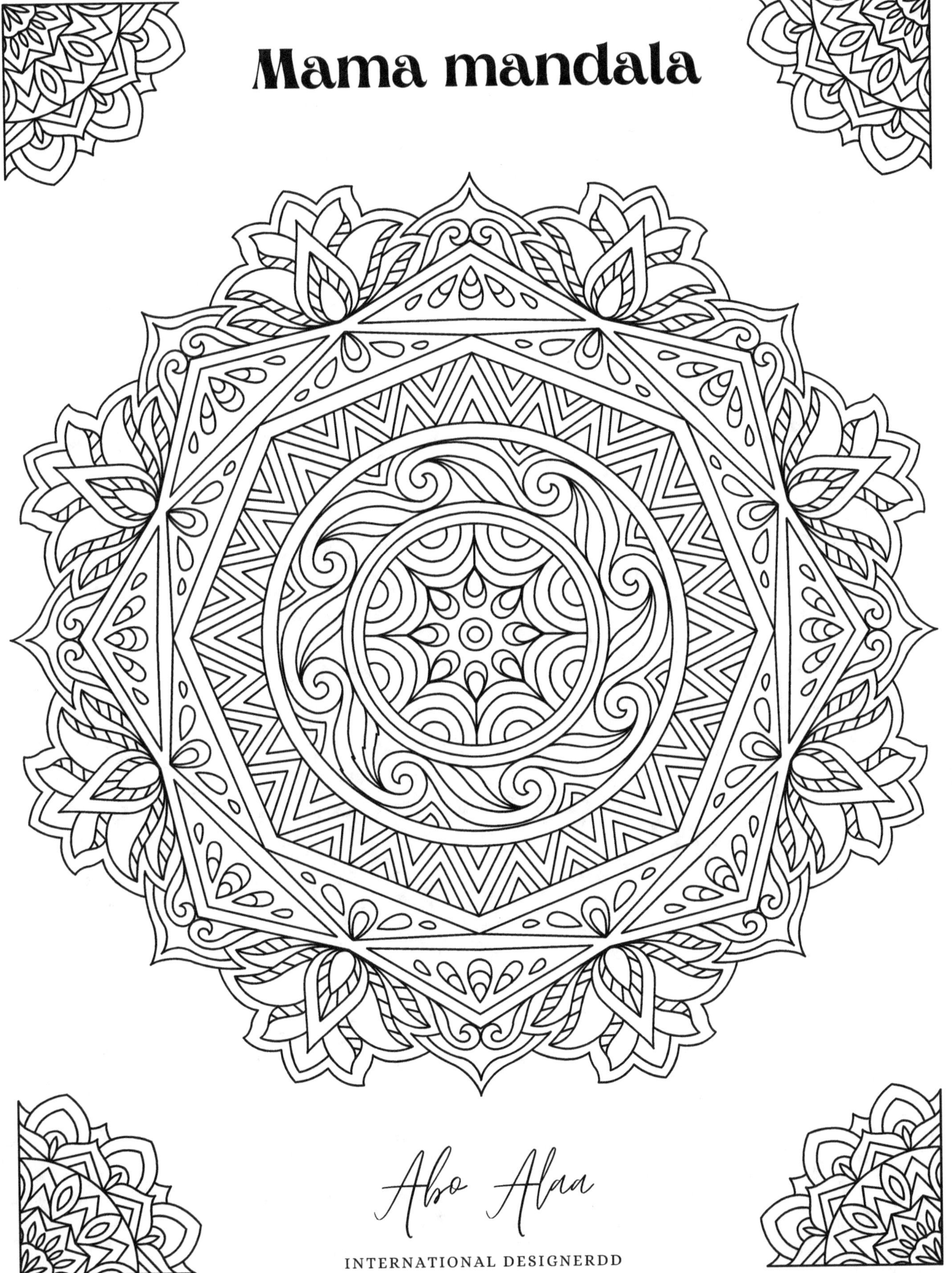

Abo Alaa

INTERNATIONAL DESIGNERDD

*Abo Alaa*

# INTERNATIONAL DESIGNERDD

# Mama mandala

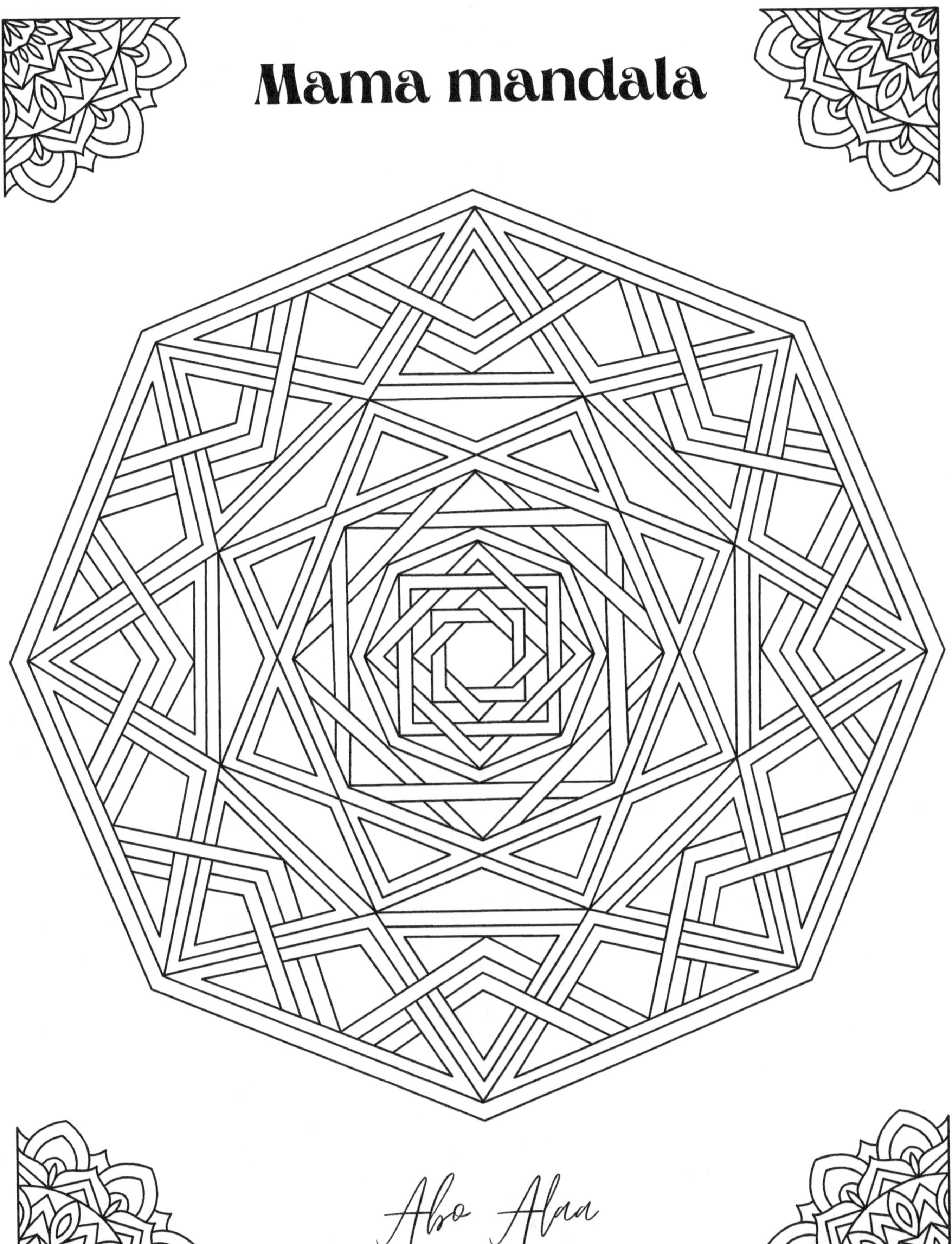

# Abo Alaa

INTERNATIONAL DESIGNERDD

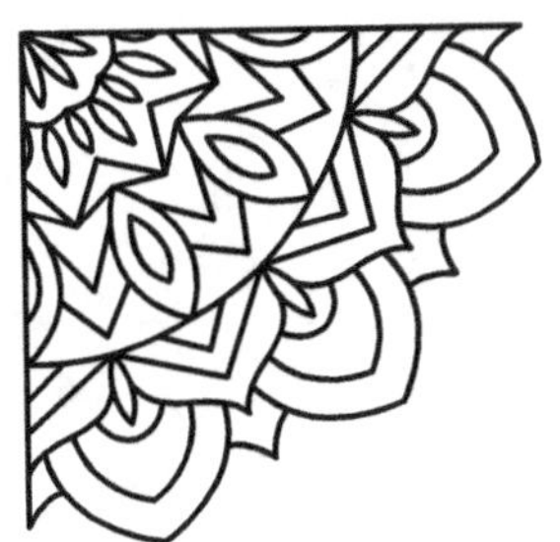

# Mama mandala

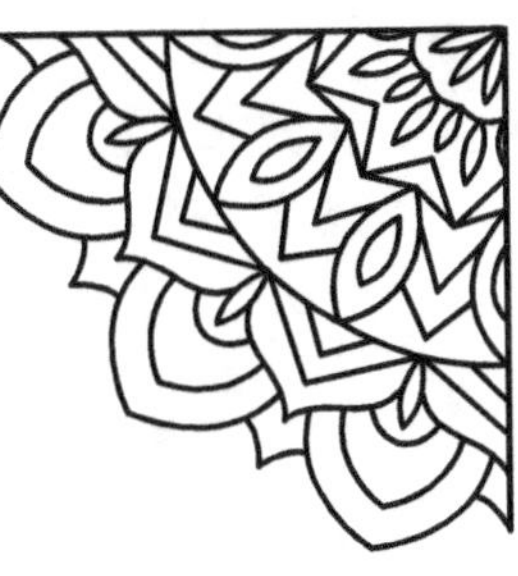

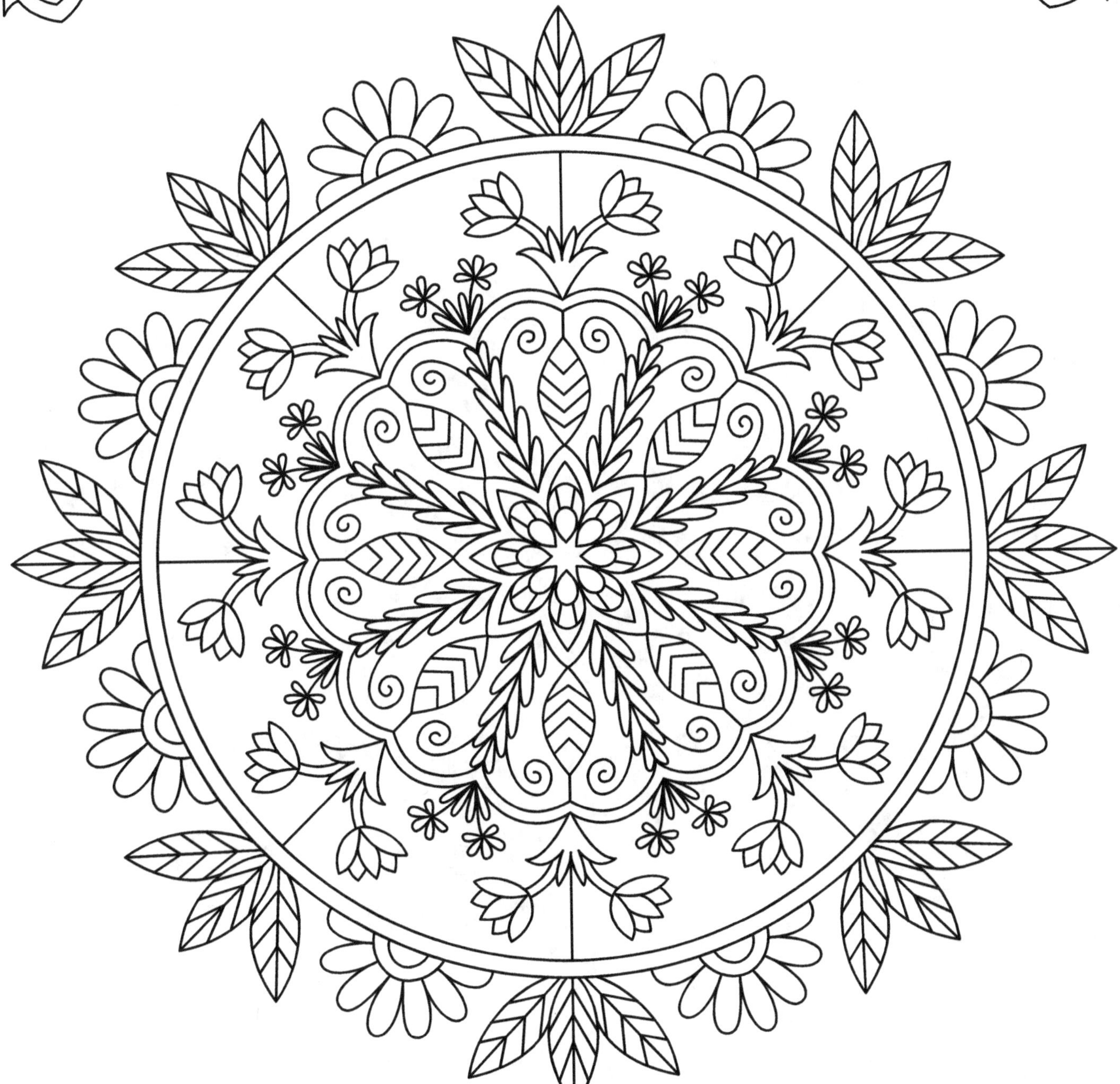

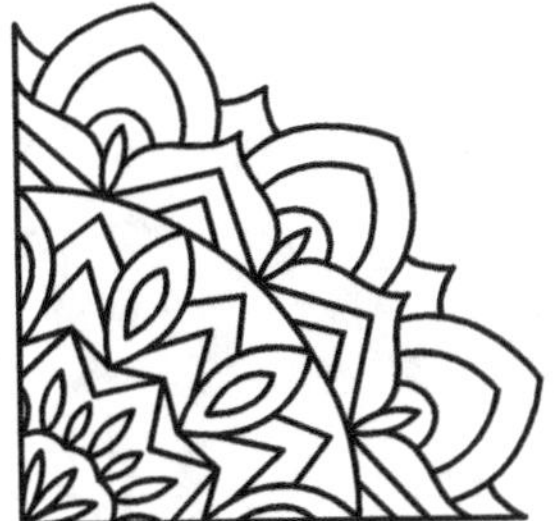

Abo Alaa

INTERNATIONAL DESIGNERDD

# Abo Alaa

INTERNATIONAL DESIGNERDD

# Mama mandala

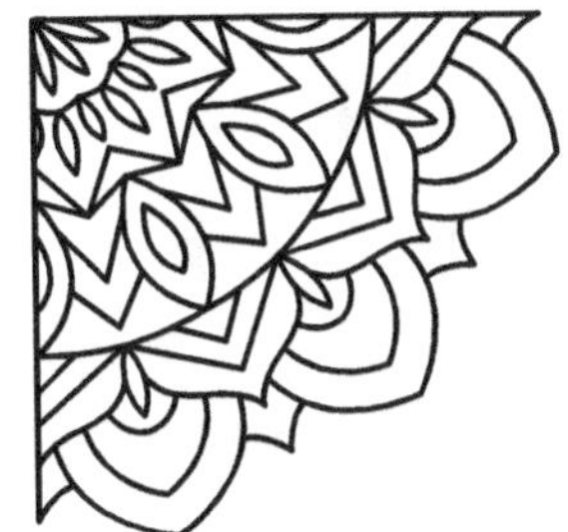
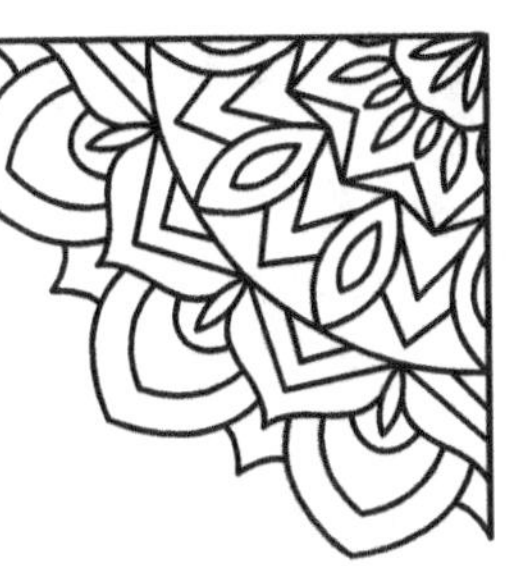
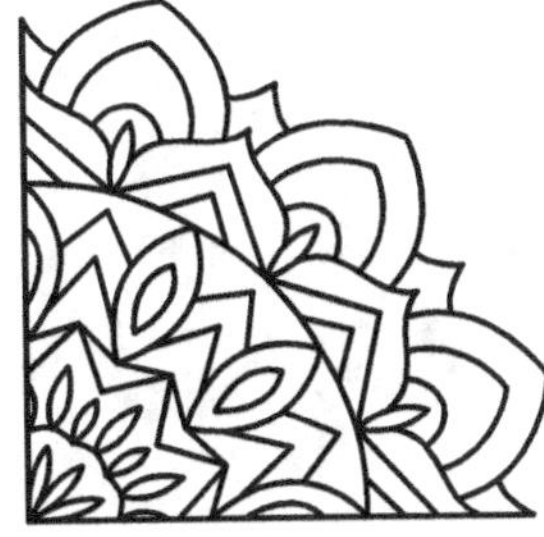

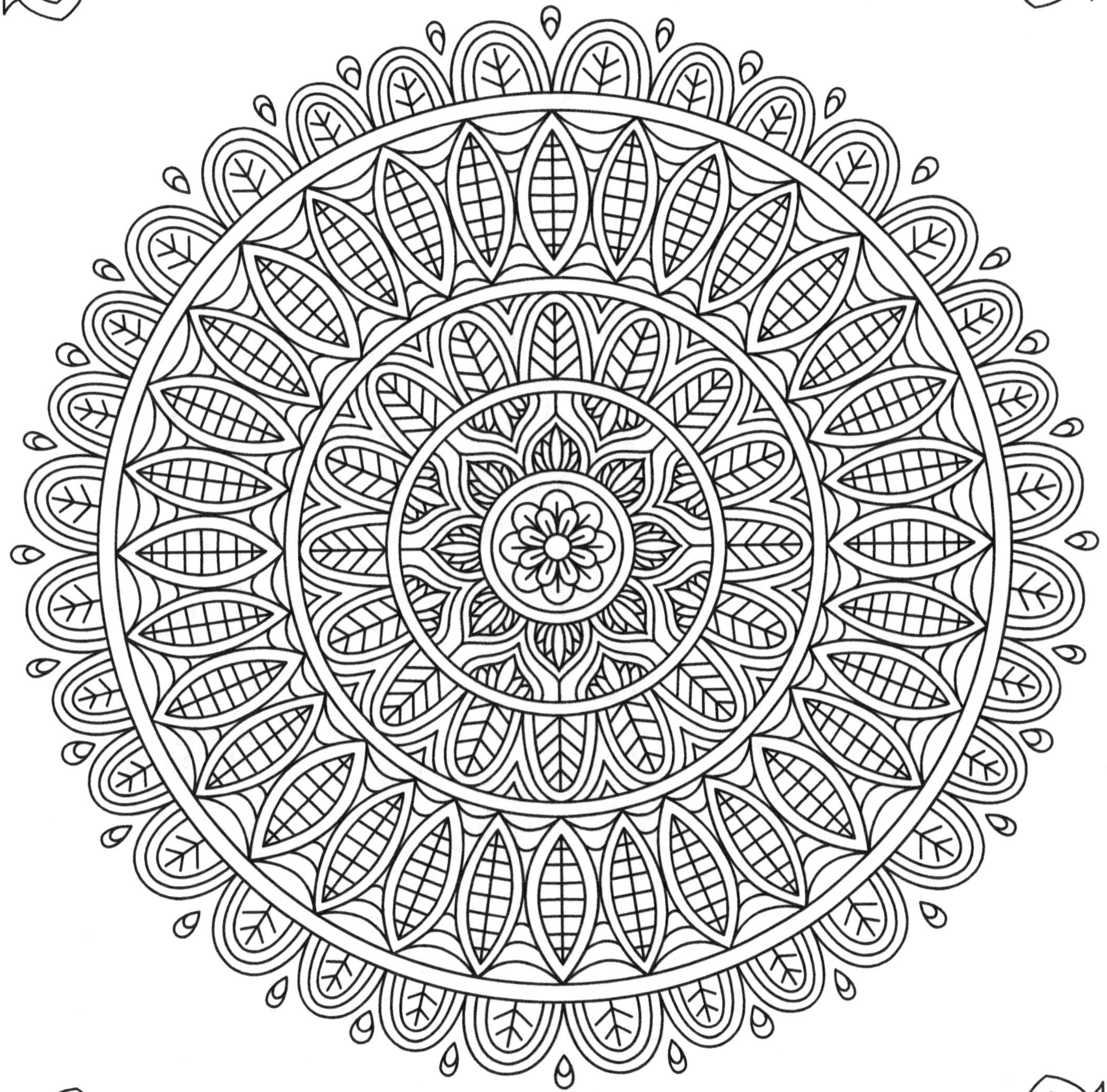

Abo Alaa

INTERNATIONAL DESIGNERDD

# Abo Alaa

INTERNATIONAL DESIGNERDD

# Mama mandala

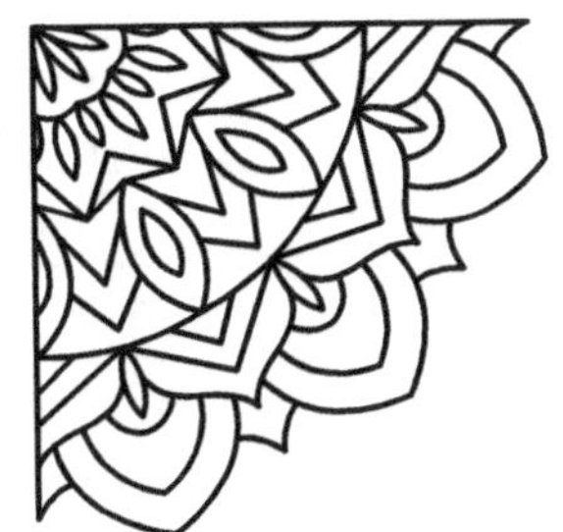
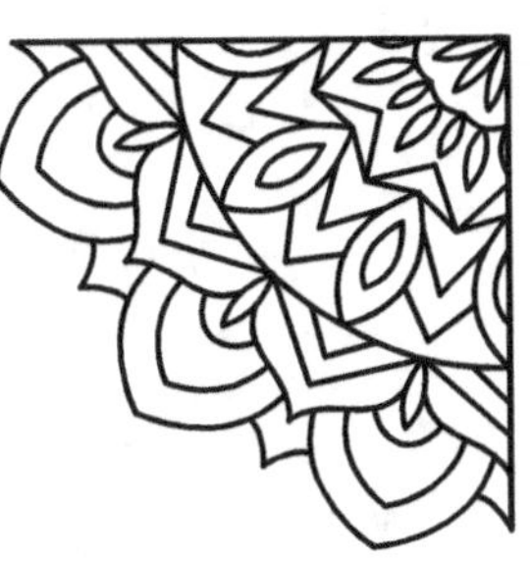
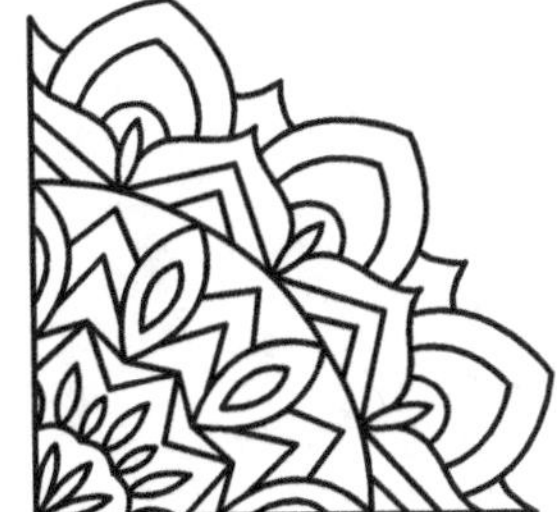

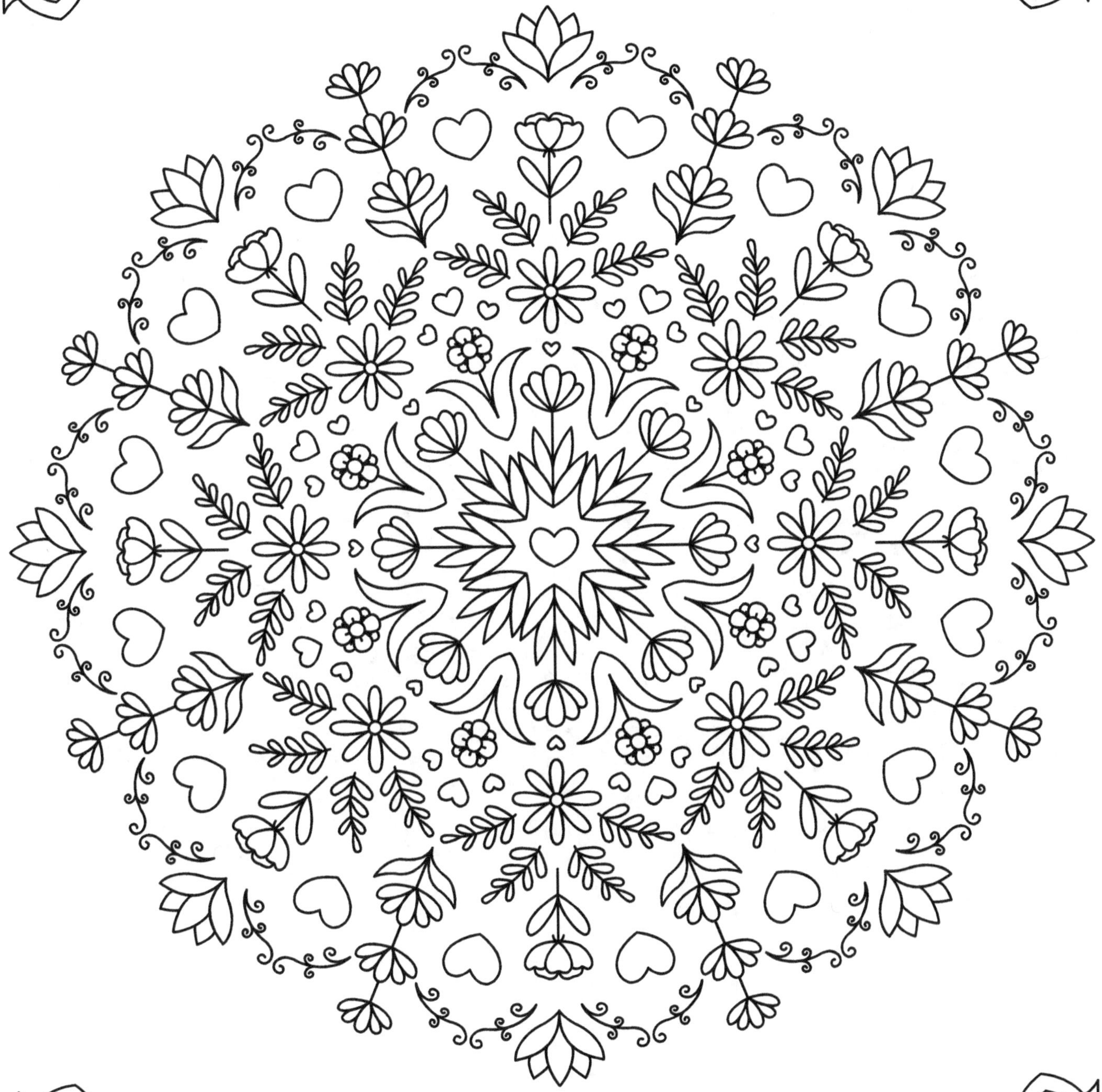

Abo Alaa

INTERNATIONAL DESIGNERDD

Abo Alaa
INTERNATIONAL DESIGNERDD

# Mama mandala

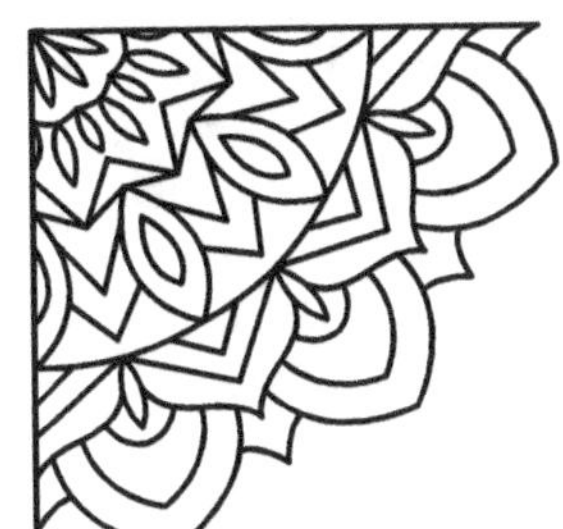
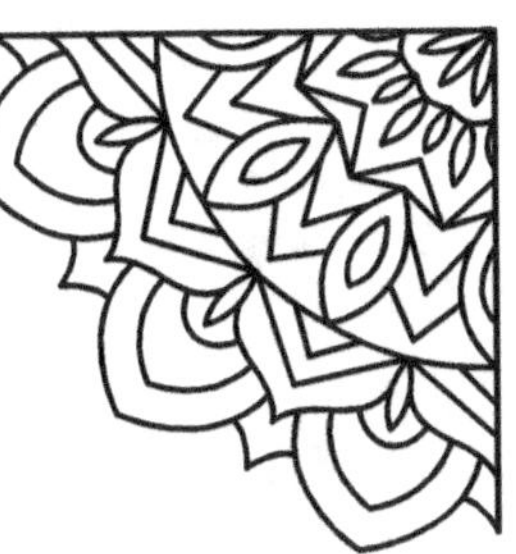
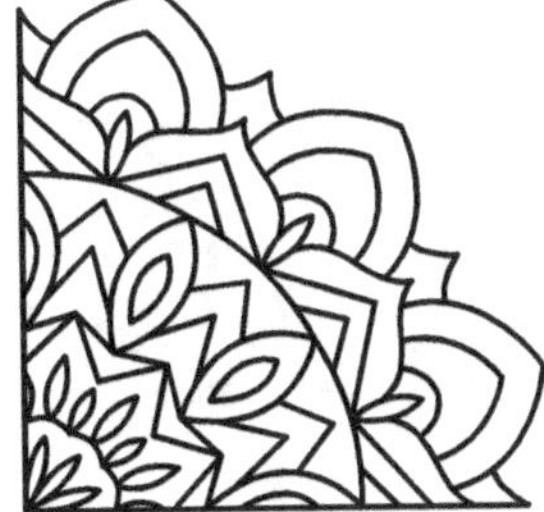
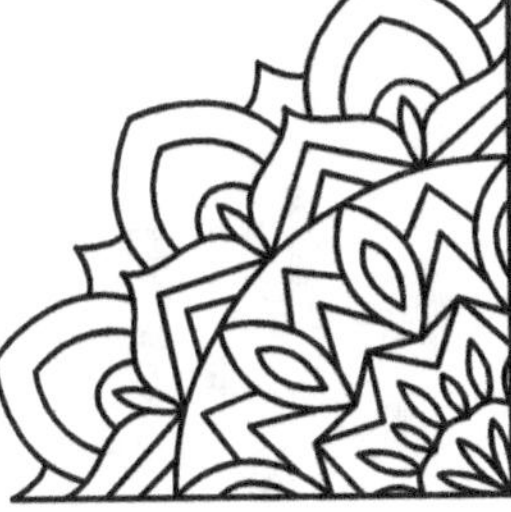

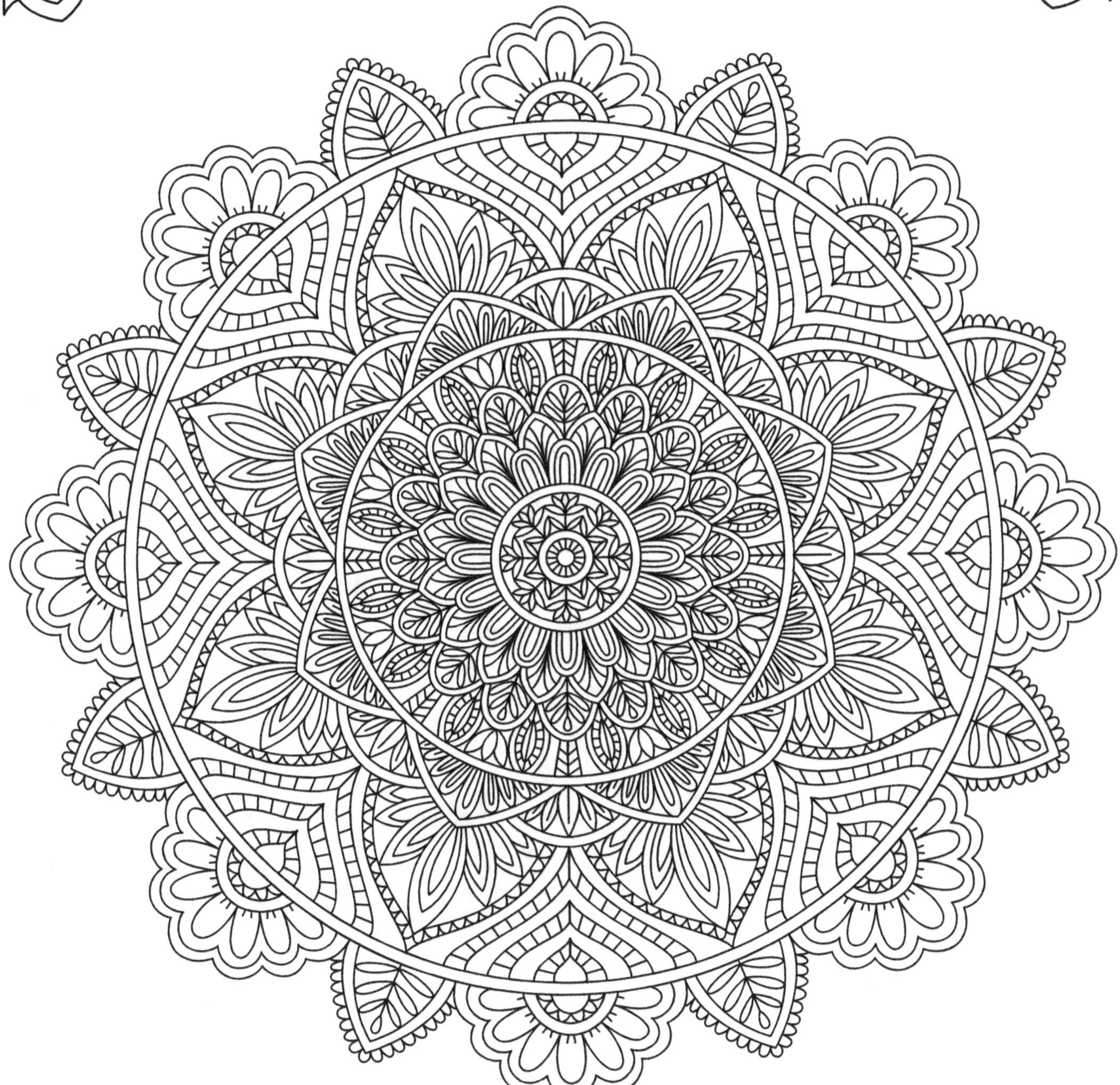

Abo Alaa

INTERNATIONAL DESIGNERDD

# Abo Alaa

INTERNATIONAL DESIGNERDD

# Mama mandala

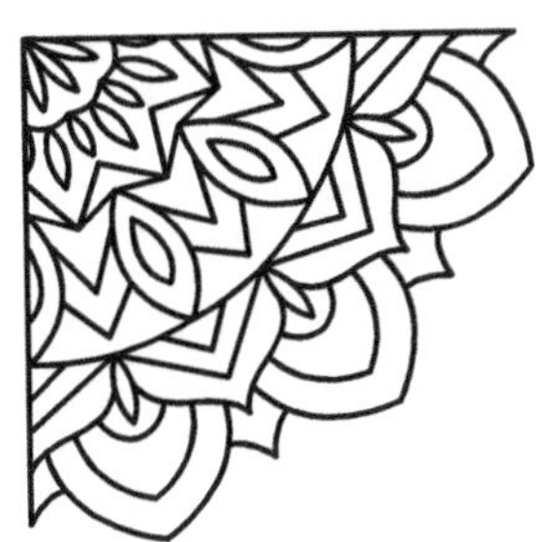
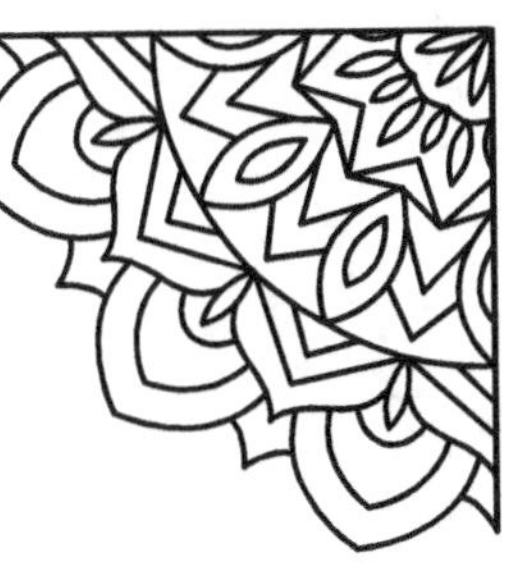
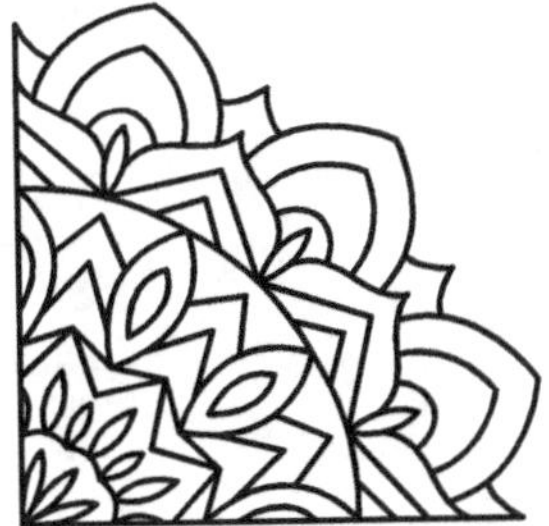
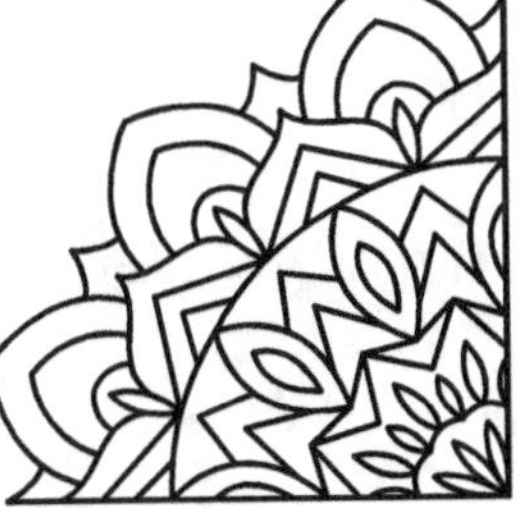

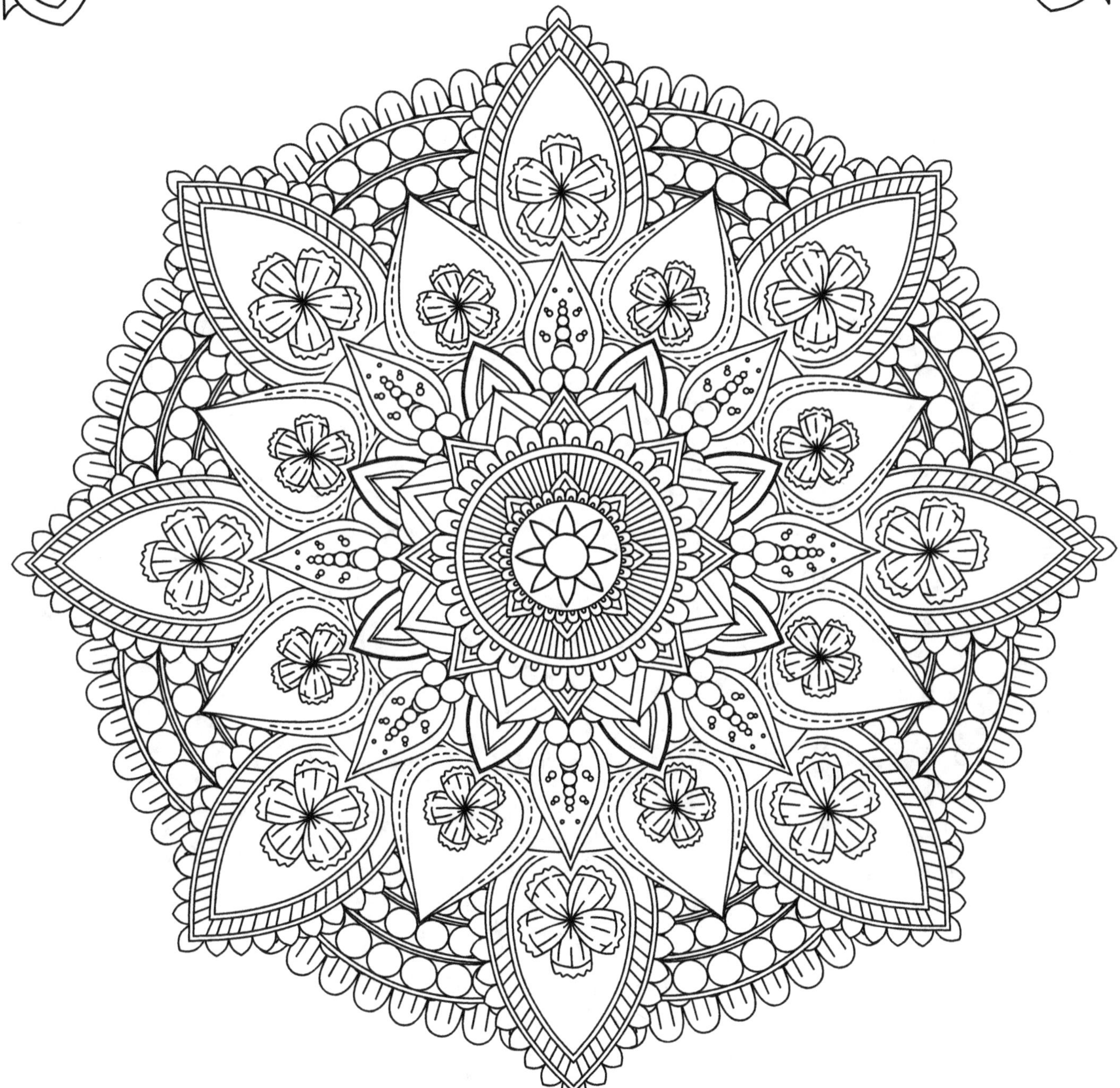

Abo Alaa

INTERNATIONAL DESIGNERDD

Abo Alaa

INTERNATIONAL DESIGNERDD

# Mama mandala

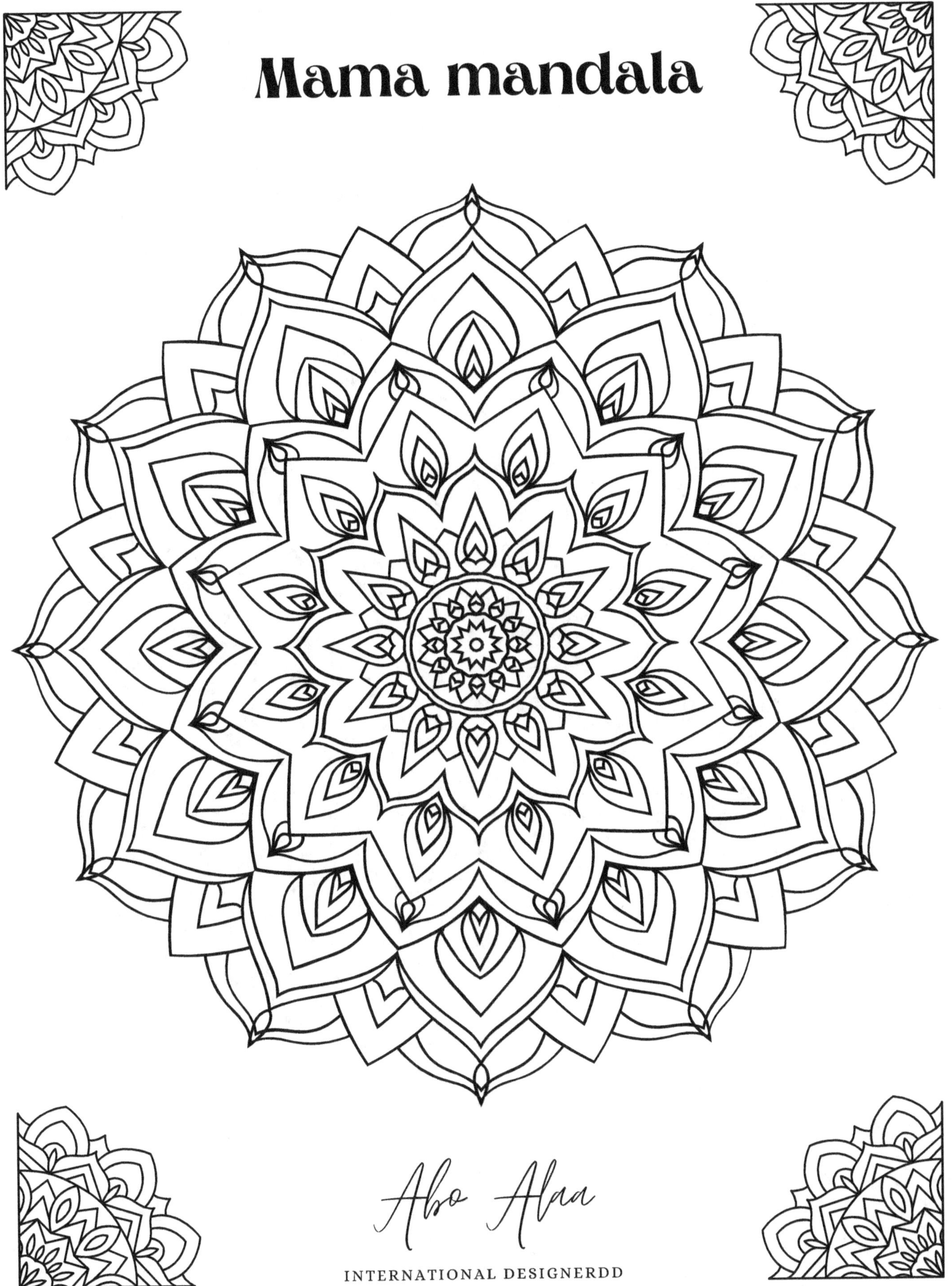

# Abo Alaa

INTERNATIONAL DESIGNERDD

# Mama mandala

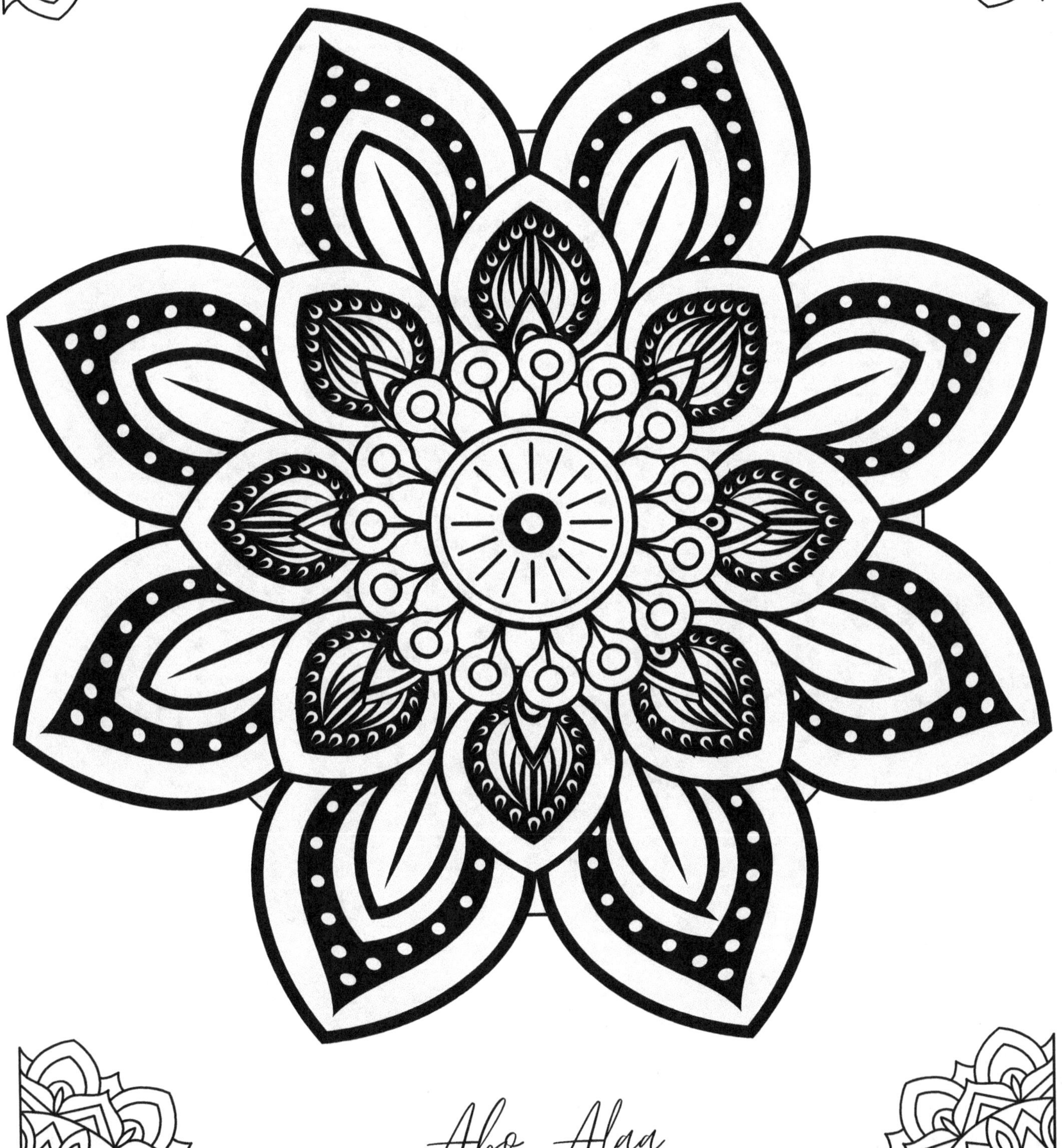

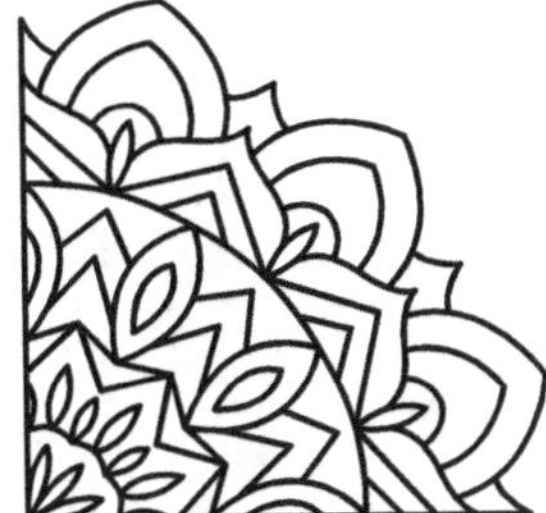

*Abo Alaa*

INTERNATIONAL DESIGNERDD

# Abo Alaa

INTERNATIONAL DESIGNERDD

# Mama mandala

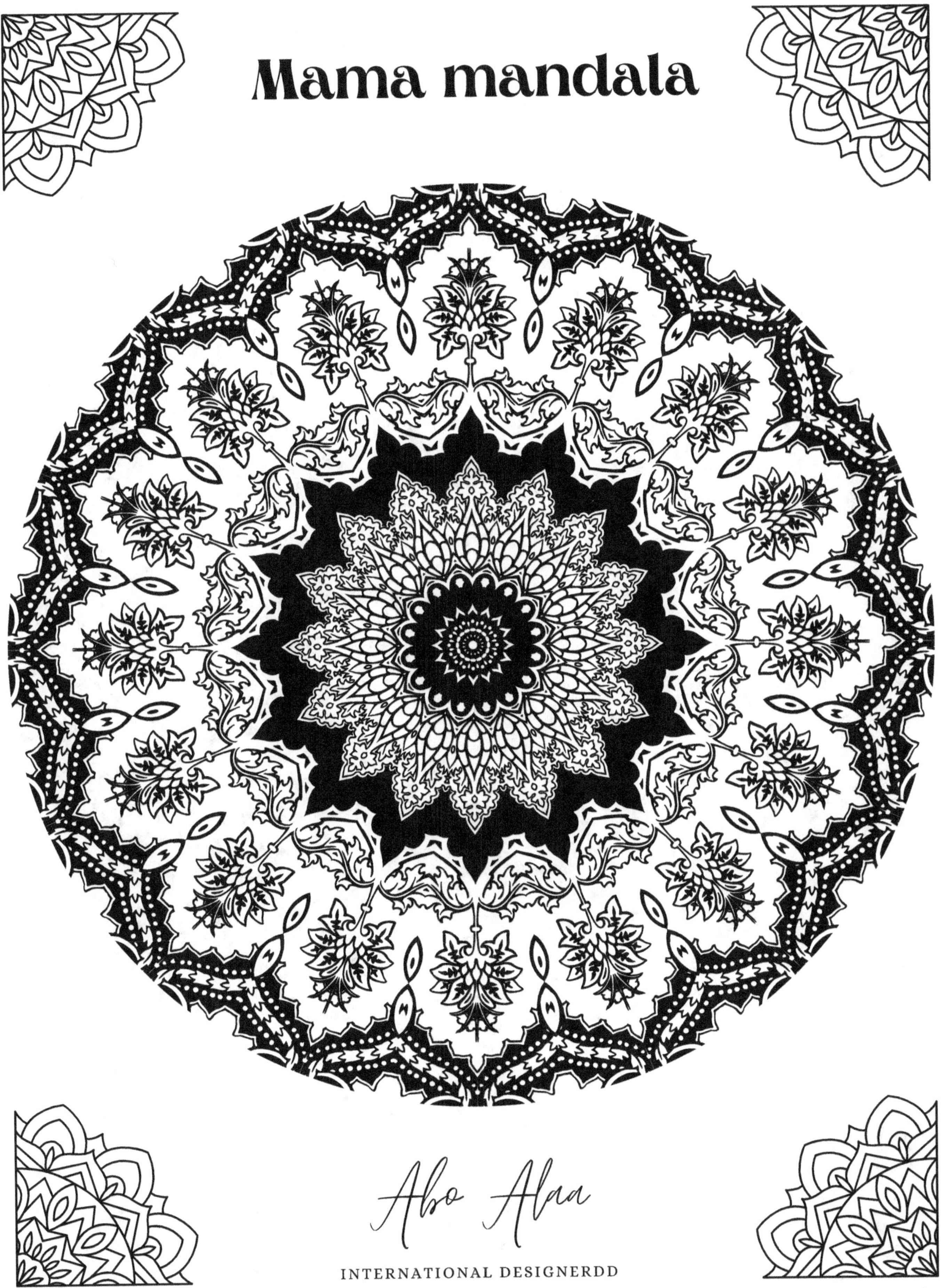

*Abo Alaa*

INTERNATIONAL DESIGNERDD

# Abo Alaa

INTERNATIONAL DESIGNERDD

# Mama mandala

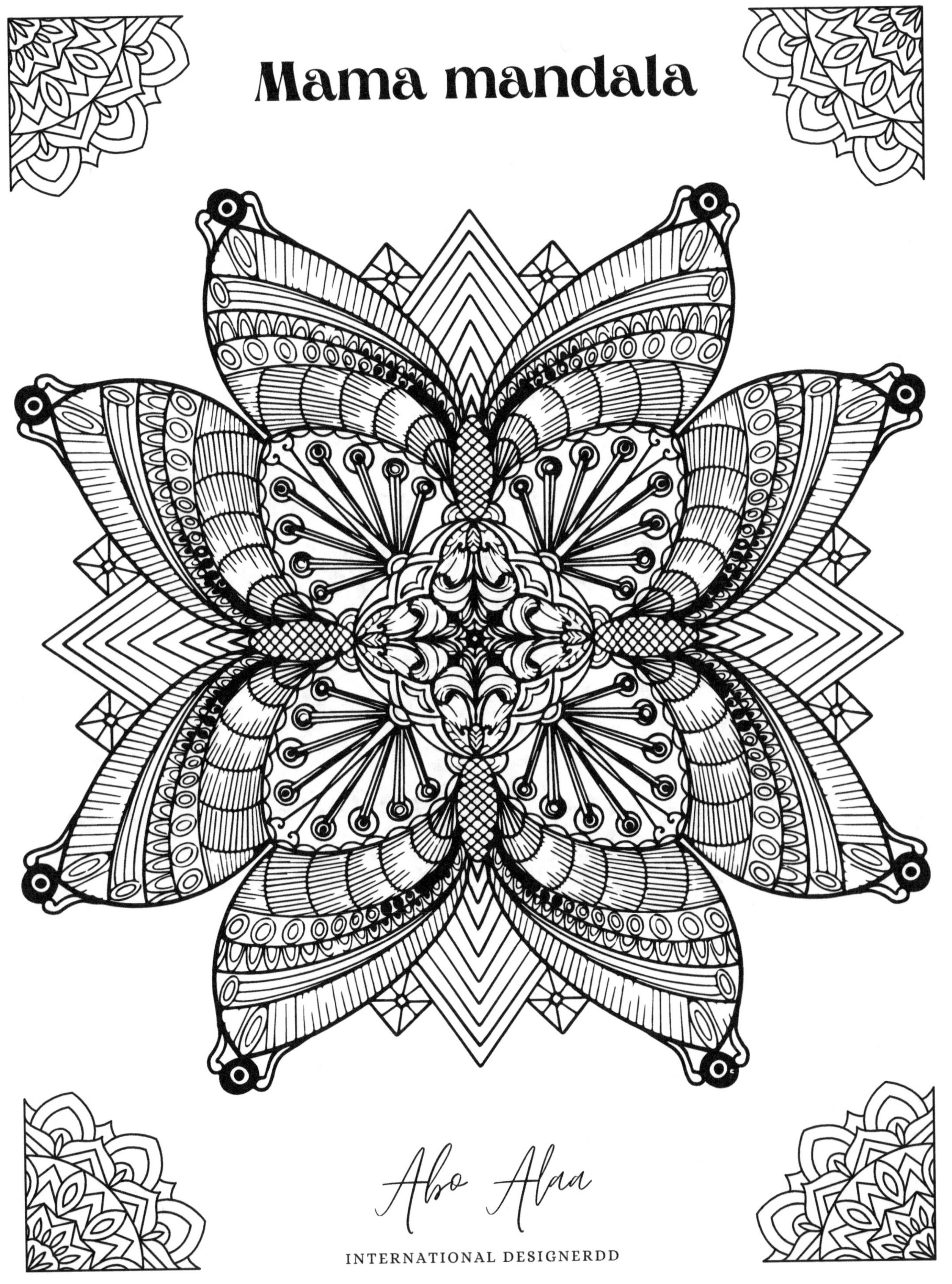



INTERNATIONAL DESIGNERDD

Abo Alaa

INTERNATIONAL DESIGNERDD

# Mama mandala

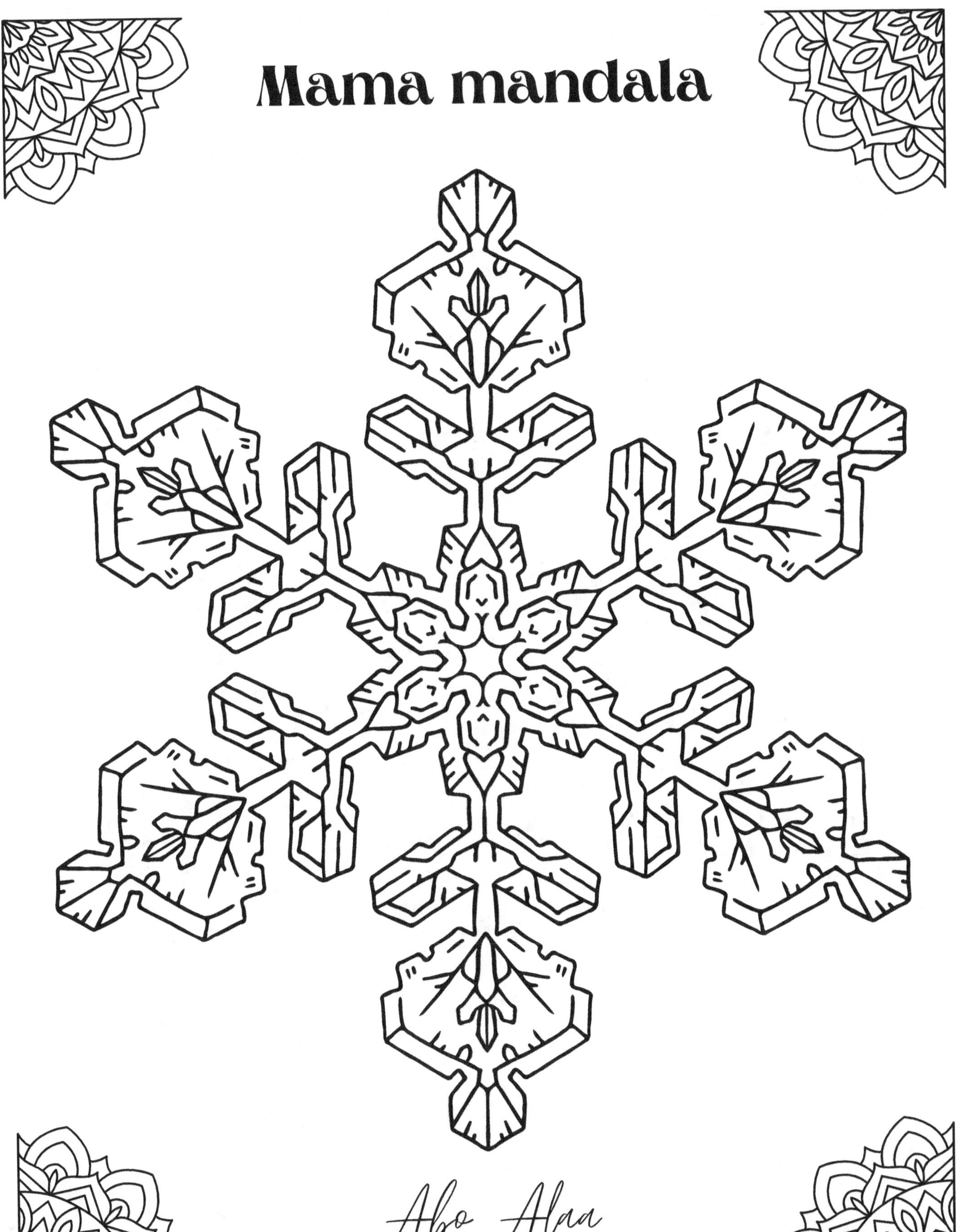

# Abo Alaa

INTERNATIONAL DESIGNERDD

# Mama mandala

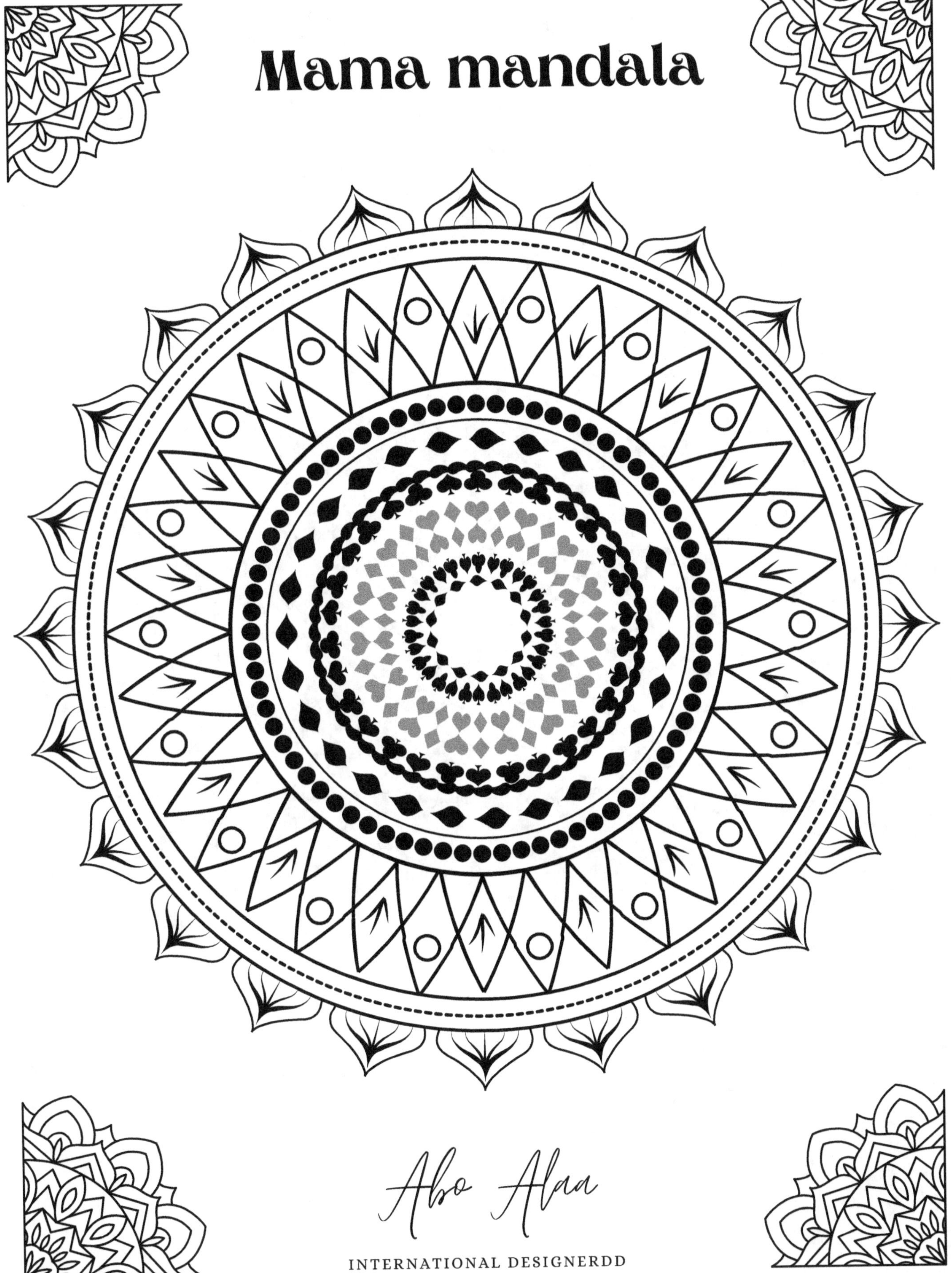



INTERNATIONAL DESIGNERDD

# Abo Alaa

INTERNATIONAL DESIGNERDD

# Mama mandala

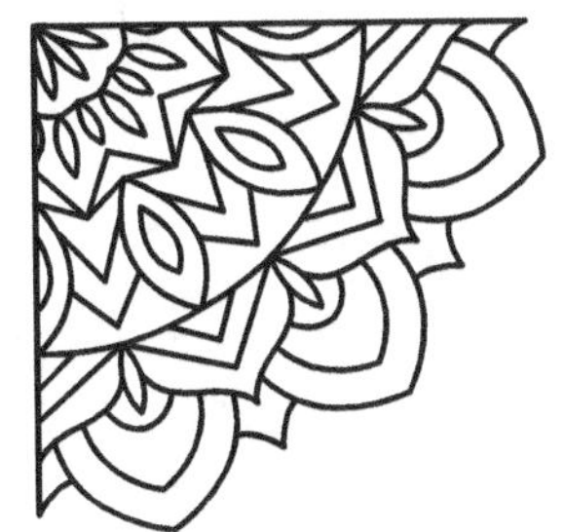
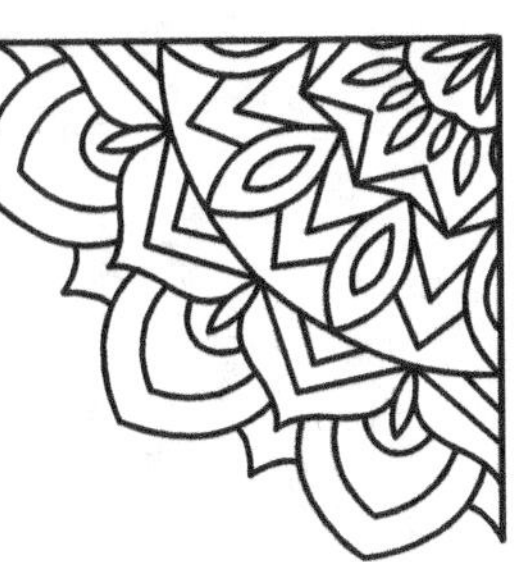
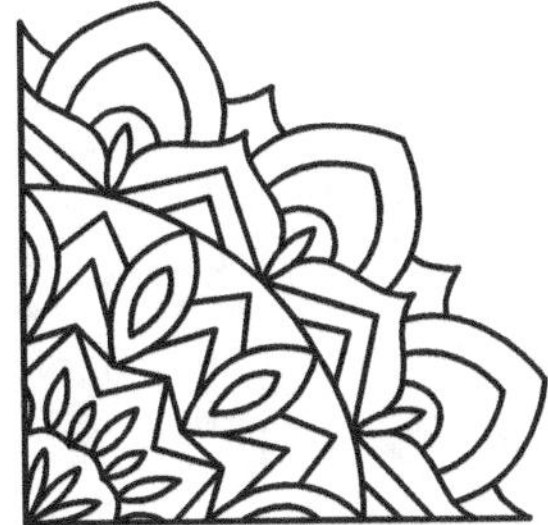

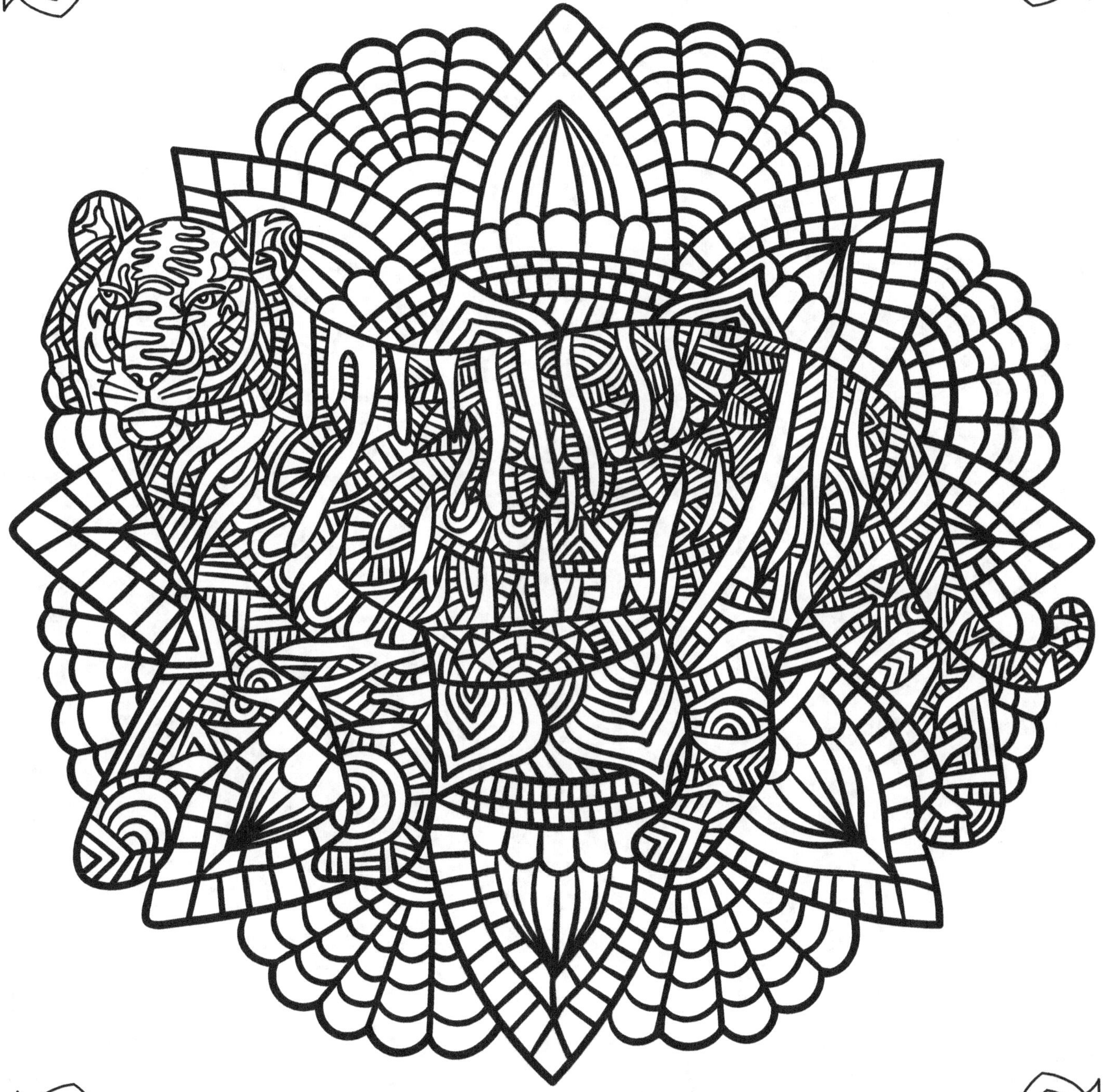

*Abo Alaa*

INTERNATIONAL DESIGNERDD

# Abo Alaa

INTERNATIONAL DESIGNERDD

# Mama mandala

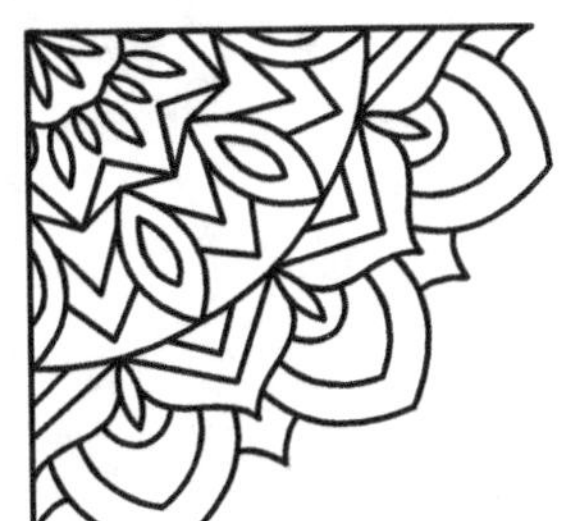
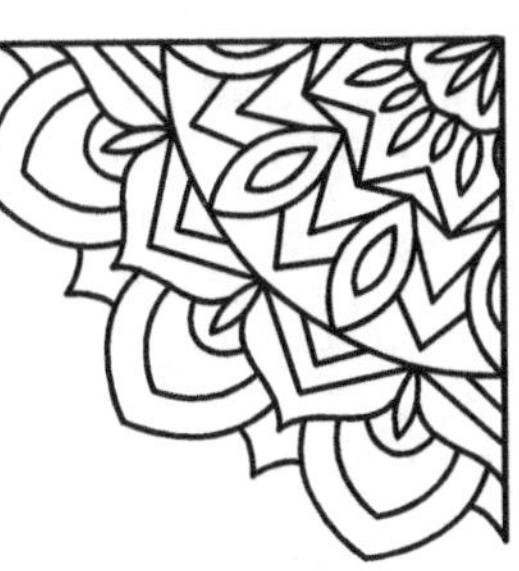
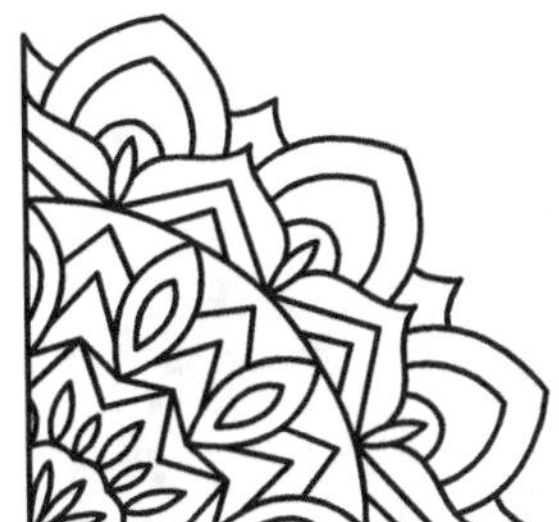

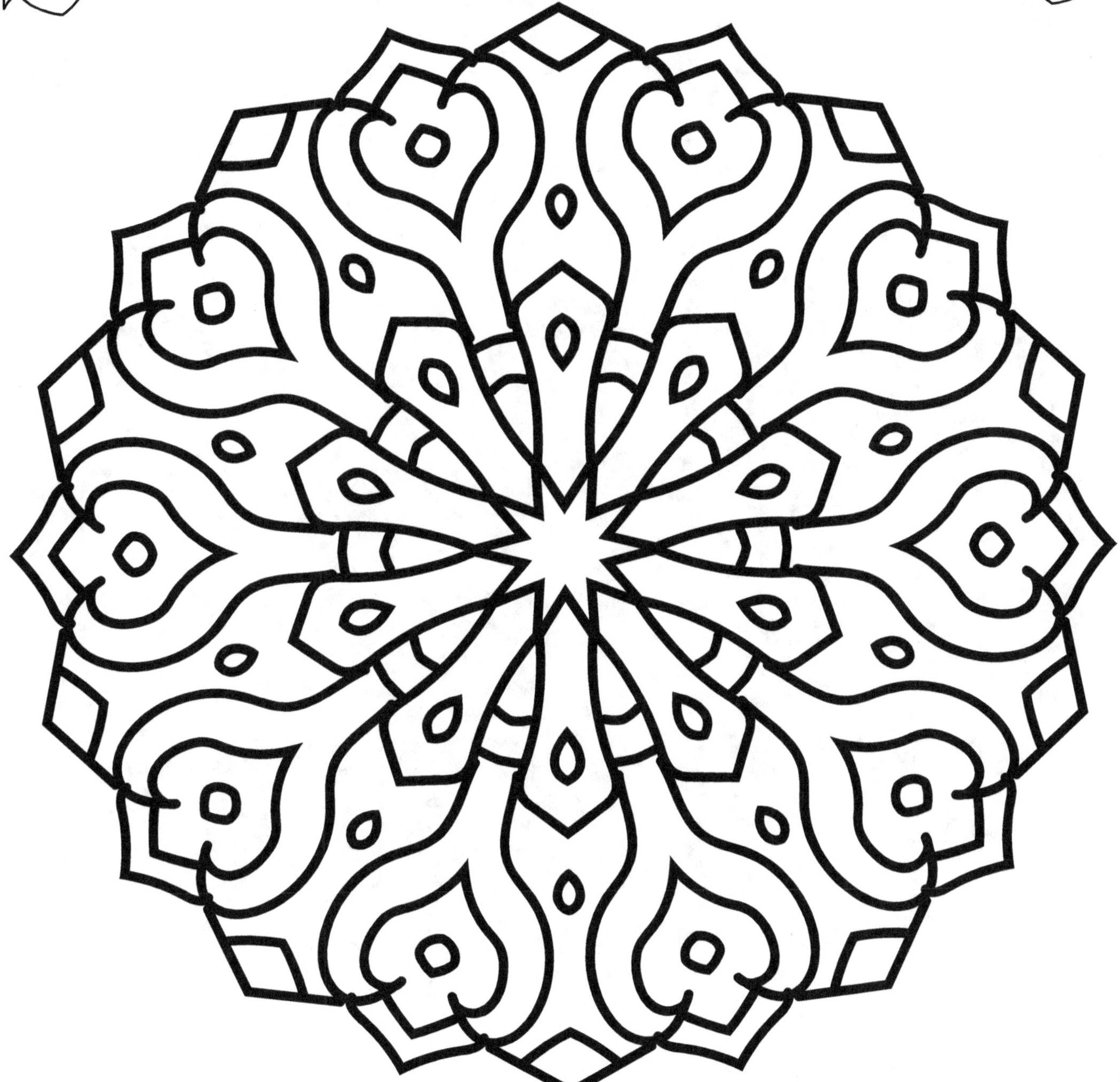

*Abo Alaa*

INTERNATIONAL DESIGNERDD

# Abo Alaa

INTERNATIONAL DESIGNERDD

# Mama mandala

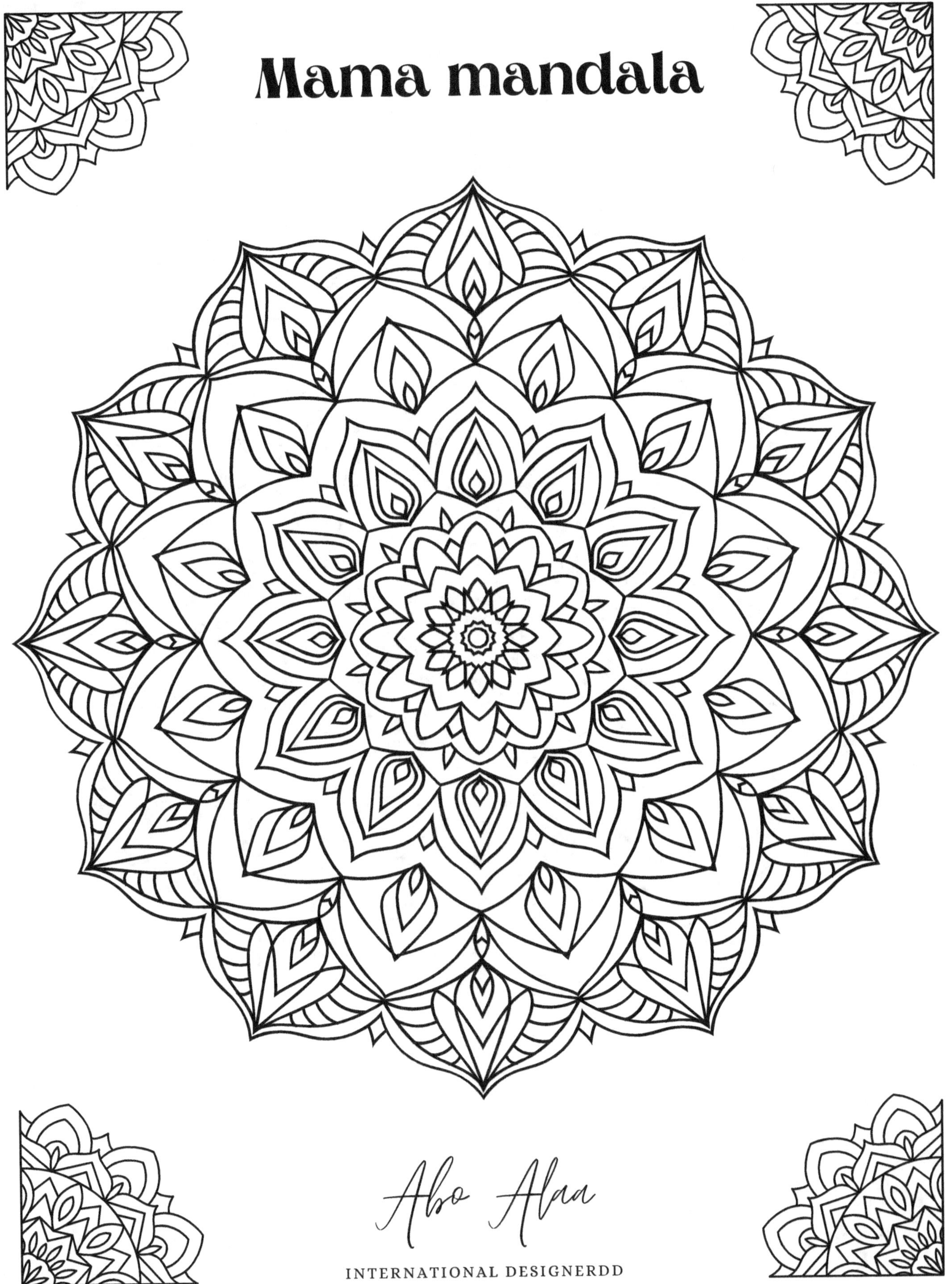

# Abo Alaa

INTERNATIONAL DESIGNERDD

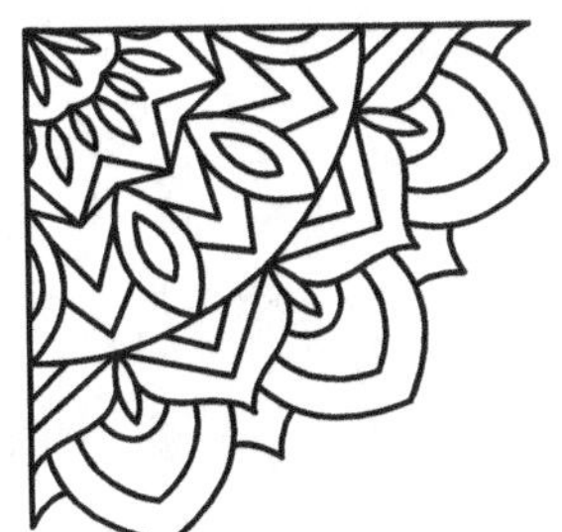
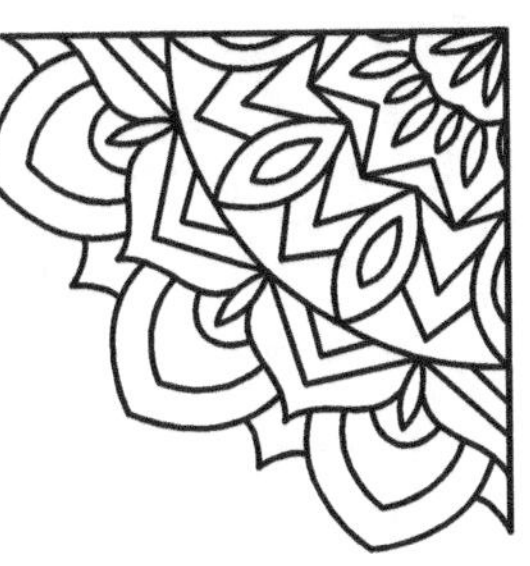

# Mama mandala

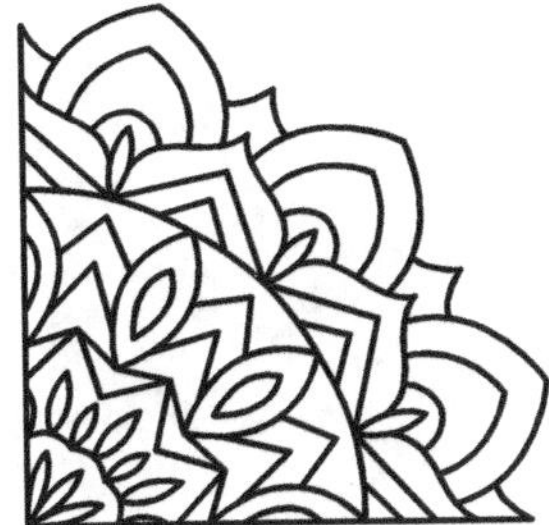
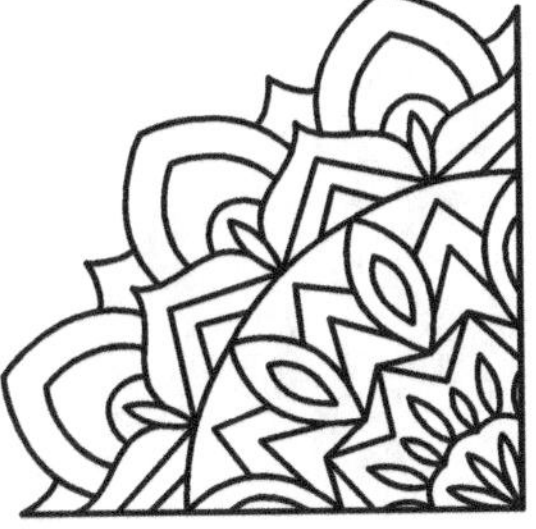

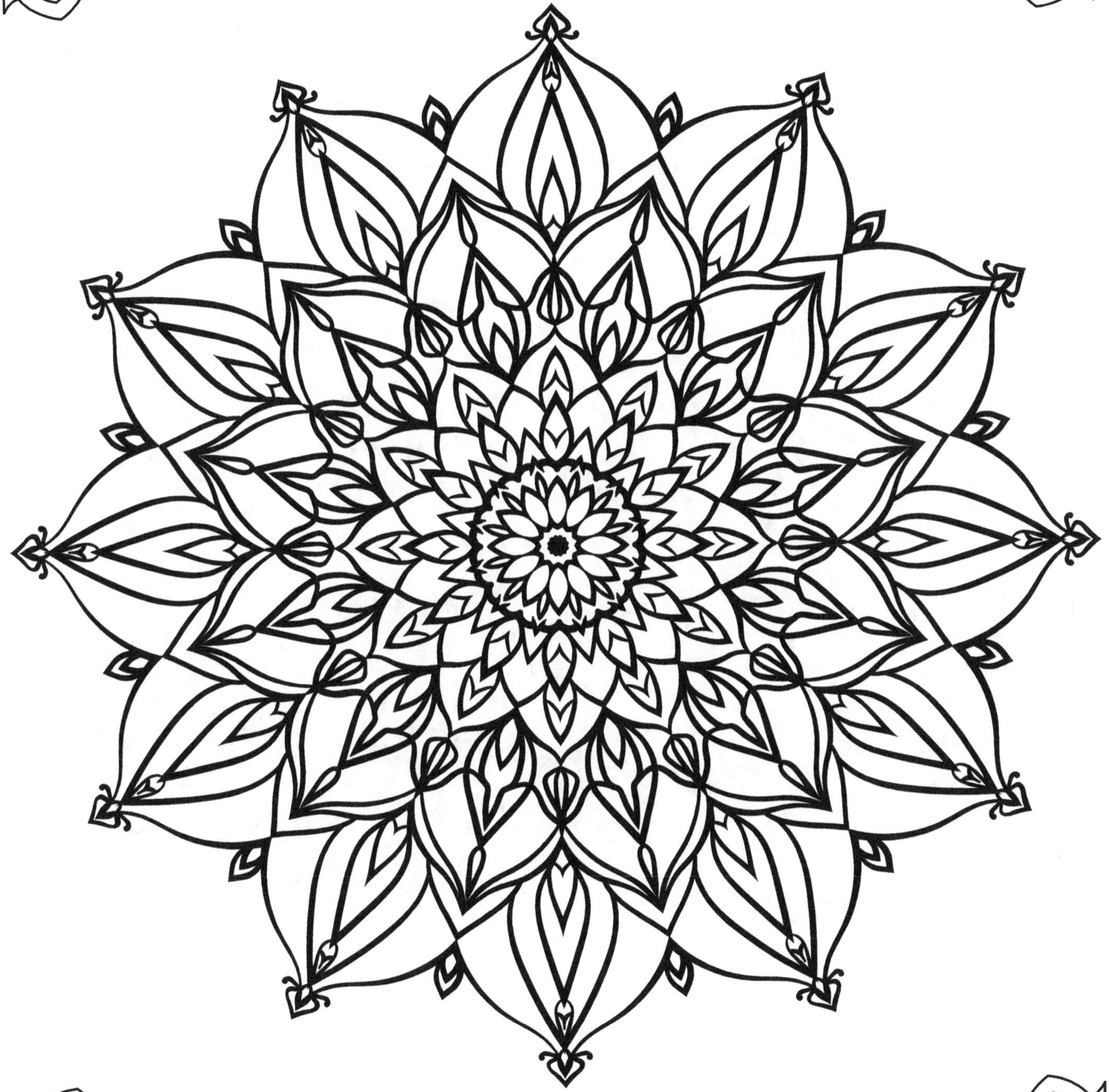

Abo Alaa

INTERNATIONAL DESIGNERDD

# Abo Alaa

INTERNATIONAL DESIGNERDD